ranch of th
th

The Race
to the North

The Race to the North

Rivalry and Record-Breaking in the Golden Age of Steam

David Wragg

WHARNCLIFFE
TRANSPORT

First published in Great Britain in 2013 by
WHARNCLIFFE TRANSPORT
an imprint of
Pen & Sword Books Ltd
47 Church Street
Barnsley
South Yorkshire
S70 2AS

ISBN 978-1-84884-772-9

Typeset by Concept, Huddersfield, West Yorkshire.
Printed and bound in England by CPI Group (UK) Ltd, Croydon, CR0 4YY.

Pen & Sword Books Ltd incorporates the imprints of Pen & Sword Aviation,
Pen & Sword Family History, Pen & Sword Maritime, Pen & Sword Military,
Pen & Sword Discovery, Wharncliffe Local History, Wharncliffe True Crime,
Wharncliffe Transport, Pen & Sword Select, Pen & Sword Military Classics,
nember When, Seaforth Publishing and
Publishing.

: Sword titles please contact
BOOKS LIMITED
th Yorkshire, S70 2AS, England
en-and-sword.co.uk
n-and-sword.co.uk

Contents

Acknowledgements

In researching any book such as this, an author is always grateful to those who have written on the subject in the past and especially the contemporary accounts to be found in places such as the Search Engine of the National Railway Museum of York, where the back copies of many railway magazines, including *The Railway News*, are to be found. I would like to thank the staff of the NRM for their unfailing helpfulness and cheerfulness.

David Wragg
Edinburgh
March 2012

Introduction

Imagine boarding a train, while on the other side, or in railway terms 'face', of the platform sits another train. Both leave together at exactly the same time, but then attempt to race each other to the terminus at the end of the line. Fantasy? Of course it is. It could never really happen like that, at least, not quite like that. Yet, in place of another platform substitute another terminus, less than a mile away, and the fantasy becomes reality.

In the late nineteenth century, some of Britain's leading mainline railway companies threw caution to the wind in an attempt to provide the fastest passenger express services between London and Scotland. These became known as the 'races to the north' and came in two phases, in 1888 and 1895, with the first set of races being to Edinburgh, while the later set was spurred by the new bridges across the Firth of Forth and Firth of Tay and, naturally, Aberdeen was the objective.

This is the story of races on the railways in the late nineteenth and early twentieth century, including that between the London & South Western and Great Western railways that resulted in a serious fatal accident at Salisbury, which focusses mainly on the determination of the railway companies to see who could provide the fastest schedule between London and the main Scottish cities.

The rivalry and its intensity was surprising given that previously the companies had seemed content to coexist and had even, at one stage, agreed that trains to Glasgow should only run from Euston while Edinburgh was to be served only from King's Cross. Even after it was agreed that both these London termini could serve the two main Scottish cities, revenues were apportioned. The East Coast Main Line (ECML) soon became the faster route, with the day express between King's Cross and Edinburgh an hour quicker than that from Euston, but the London & North Western Railway (LNWR), economy-minded at the time, objected to fast running as the locomotives consumed too much coal. Looking back over more than a century, it is important to bear in mind that not everyone realised that speed was important or even a marketing advantage, as an alternative to the road coach and later the railway was travel by sea, with both the East and West Coast routes well served by small liners, sometimes carrying up to 300 passengers, and also by cargo ships with accommodation for a limited number of passengers.

Until the Tay and the Forth were bridged, north of Edinburgh the ECML had to transfer its passengers to ferries and its goods wagons to barges to continue northwards to Aberdeen. With the backing of the other companies engaged in the East Coast group of companies, the North British Railway constructed a bridge across the Firth of Tay and planned a bridge across the Firth of Forth so that the rivalry between the East and West Coast companies could extend to Dundee, Perth and Aberdeen. Disaster struck on a stormy night, 28 December 1879, when the Tay Bridge collapsed as a train was running northwards across it, with the loss of all seventy-two people aboard.

The Tay Bridge was replaced and a different engineer designed a bridge across the Firth of Forth, finally allowing the East Coast companies to become the fastest to Aberdeen. The city was a prime target for the railways because the heavy indentations of the Firth of Tay and Firth of Forth meant that a fast direct route south did not exist, yet the heavy fish traffic, and the prime agricultural produce of the surrounding area, as well as passenger traffic, indicated that the route would be viable.

Even before the two bridges opened, the cosy arrangement between the East and West Coast groups of companies had come under attack in 1876, when the Midland Railway completed its line to Scotland via Settle and Carlisle. Its line was longer and slower than the two existing lines, but the Midland had admitted third-class passengers to all of its trains and improved their lot by abolishing second-class whilst scrapping its small stock of third-class carriages. By contrast, the East Coast service was first-class only until 1887, the year that the second Tay Bridge opened.

The lack of a through route north of Edinburgh was not the only problem that had affected the East Coast line. For many years, at York and then at Newcastle, trains had to reverse rather than run through the stations.

Before the Forth Bridge was completed in 1890, in May 1888 the West Coast companies suddenly announced that from 2 June their fastest express would run from Euston to Edinburgh in nine hours, the same time as that from King's Cross. The East Coast companies responded by cutting the through journey time to eight hours, which the West Coast matched from 1 August. On 13 August, the East Coast schedule was cut to 7hr 45min, but on that day the train reached Edinburgh in 7hr 27min. Then, as suddenly as it started, the racing stopped and the two rival groups agreed minimum journey times for their trains.

This was just the first of the railway races to the north. Once the Forth and new Tay bridges were completed, the through journey time to Dundee and Aberdeen was cut, to the benefit of the East Coast line. This was the spark that set off yet another 'race', between the overnight trains from London to Aberdeen. The timetable was ignored in the interest of getting the trains to their destination in the shortest possible time, but after the East Coast companies decided to stop the 'race', on the night of 23/24 August 1895, the West Coast train ran the 540 miles from Euston to Aberdeen at an average speed of 63.3mph.

While the idea of two rival trains waiting to depart from opposite sides of a platform was fanciful, something similar did arise on the races to Aberdeen. The first train to pass Kinnaber Junction was first into Aberdeen, and so it happened that on occasion the passengers and crew of the losing train would see their rival steaming by.

The irony of the situation was that after the 'races' stopped, the companies agreed on a leisurely eight and a half-hour schedule between London and both Edinburgh and Glasgow for day trains, even if non-stop, something that survived until 1932 before once again schedules were accelerated so that Edinburgh and Glasgow could be reached in just six and a half hours from King's Cross and Euston.

First to the North

The West Coast route was the first to open between London and Scotland, running via Preston and Carlisle, completed in 1858 and with through trains worked jointly by the London & North Western Railway and the Caledonian Railway. It was followed in 1862 by the East Coast route via York and Newcastle, in which the main participants were the Great Northern, North Eastern and North British railways. Both routes served Edinburgh and Glasgow, and while revenues were apportioned as the result of agreements made between 1851 and 1856, there was competition between them. The ECML soon became the faster, with the day express between King's Cross and Edinburgh an hour quicker than that from Euston, although, as already mentioned, the LNWR at the time objected to fast running.

The races then ended between London and Scotland. On the plus side, it showed just how performance, if not the passengers' sleep, could be enhanced, but on the debit side the trains used were lightly loaded and sometimes double-headed, while all other traffic had to give way to allow the racers priority. Indeed, the loads became progressively smaller as the races continued and winning became a matter of honour.

Racing Rivals
The railway companies, even before the grouping of 1923, could be said to be localized monopolies with competition at the edges. A glance at the railway map shows that between several destinations, more than one route existed. While the most lucrative of these, apart from the lines between London and Scotland, would seem to have been between London and Birmingham or Manchester, it was between London and Exeter that the first race occurred, between the London & South Western Railway (LSWR), running from Waterloo, and the alliance of the Great Western (GWR), running from Paddington, and the Bristol & Exeter, starting in 1862. In 1868, the Midland Railway managed to compete with the London & North Western between London and Manchester, and, from 1880, with the Great Northern between London and Leeds and Bradford, for which an expensive line between Kettering and Northampton was constructed.

The LSWR and the GWR then competed, between London and Plymouth, for the prestigious boat train traffic, with passengers joining or leaving liners at Plymouth to save a day or so steaming to London. The GWR even constructed one of its many 'cut off' routes during the early 1900s to shorten the distance to Plymouth in 1906. Many objected to the races because of the waste; not only because two companies were trying to provide the same service, but because they also deliberately ran trains that were seldom full. There was a more pressing argument against racing, however: safety! On the night of 29/30 June 1906, the up boat train from Plymouth to Waterloo, with a fresh locomotive and crew, after changing at Templecombe, ran through Salisbury at excessive speed, derailing at the eastern end of the station at 2.24am, killing twenty-four of the forty-three passengers.

As we will see, many raised the issue of safety as soon as the races started in 1888 and then again in 1895, but the irony was that, despite some of the eye-witness accounts that follow, it was not until 1896, a year after the races ended, that a high-speed accident occurred.

Glossary

Atlantic – Steam locomotive with a 4-4-2 wheel configuration.

Banker – A locomotive that is placed at the end of a train to provide assistance, either in starting or in ascending a gradient. It would not normally be connected to the train which would leave it behind as speed was gained.

'Big Four' – The four companies created from more than a hundred on grouping of the main line railways in 1923. These were, in order of size, the London, Midland & Scottish Railway (LMS); the London & North Eastern Railway (LNER); the Great Western Railway (GWR); and the Southern Railway (SR).

Bogies – Railway carriages with bogies, meaning that they are longer and larger, and of course heavier, but much more comfortable, than the early rigid four and six-wheelers.

Check – See Permanent way check, below.

Checked – A train stopped at signals, which would never be described as a 'stop' by railwaymen.

Cut-off – (1) Quoted as a percentage, this is the point in the piston stroke at which steam supply to the cylinders is stopped by closing the admission valve. The cut-off is reduced as speed increases, so that a locomotive might start off at 75 or 80 per cent cut-off, but at full speed this could be 15 per cent. (2) A new length of track built to shorten a route.

Cwt – Abbreviation for hundredweight, which is 112lb, a twentieth of an imperial ton.

Diagram – The schedule for a locomotive during its day's work.

Down – A train or the line running from London, or in Scotland from Edinburgh. Some companies used their head office as the starting point, so that the Midland Railway had 'down' for trains and lines running from its head office at Derby. In South Wales, trains ran 'down' the valleys to the coast.

Fitted – Freight train with wagons having brakes.

Four foot – The space between adjoining tracks other than on the Great Western (*see* **Six foot**).

Imbibing – A steam locomotive taking on water while stationary.

Interlocking frame – Equipment within a railway signal box that ensures that signals and points are connected so that conflicting or dangerous movements cannot be arranged.

Junior – A young railwayman under the age of twenty.

Length – The stretch of track allocated to a gang of platelayers.

Light/light engine – A locomotive running on its own without carriages or wagons. The term has nothing to do with the weight of the locomotive.

Link – A combination of duties for a group of personnel qualified to perform them. Often these included a 'top' or 'first' link whose members received the highest rates of pay and were awarded the prestige of express workings.

Mikado – A steam locomotive with a 2-8-2 wheel configuration.

Motion – The connecting rods and other mechanisms linking the cylinder with the wheels. On a two-cylinder locomotive, these were usually on the outside, but three- and four-cylinder locomotives, or those with 'inside' cylinders, had cylinders that were difficult to reach.

On time – During the period under review, a train was either on time or late, unlike today when a delay of five minutes is allowed as on time for short-distance services, and ten minutes for longer distance services.

Pacific – Steam locomotive with a 4-6-2 wheel configuration.

Permanent way check or **slack** – A temporary speed limit due to a fault with the line or during engineering work.

Pilot – A steam locomotive that provides extra power and is placed at the head of a train in front of the train locomotive. It is usually connected to the other locomotive and the train braking system. The Midland Railway was notorious for having small locomotives, so many of its trains were double-headed – the leading locomotive being the pilot.

Regulation – Control of trains within the system to ensure safety and timekeeping.

Regulator – This is the valve that regulates the flow of steam to the cylinders and in general terms serves the same function as the throttle on aircraft engines or the accelerator in a car.

Road – The track.

Signal check – When a train is halted at a signal – never stopped.

Stirling single – A locomotive with a single large driving wheel on each side, built at a time when metallurgy was insufficiently advanced to provide connecting rods that could link two driving wheels on each side. Stirling refers to the designer, Patrick Stirling. Other singles used by other companies attracted names such as the 'Midland Spinner'.

Stop – A scheduled call at a railway station or halt, but never at signals.

Timetable – The 'public timetable' which is advertised and published and available to members of the public (*see* **Working timetable**).

Unfitted – Freight train with wagons that do not have a continuous braking system and must be manually and individually hand braked on arriving at their destination.

Up – A train or line running towards London, or in Scotland towards Edinburgh. The Midland Railway was an exception with trains and lines running up towards Derby, while in South Wales trains ran 'up' the valleys from the coast.

Working timetable – The timetable used by railwaymen, never by the public. The working timetable would include timing points other than calls at stations, and in some cases the schedule might be slightly tighter than shown in the public timetable to make an on time arrival more likely.

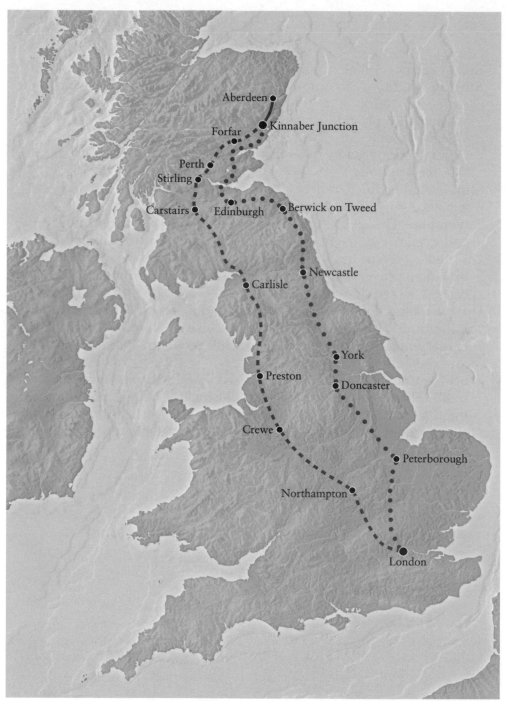

The rival routes to Aberdeen for the great race of 1895. The West Coast is shown in broken lines; the East Coast as dots. As the two routes came together at Kinnaber Junction to the south of Aberdeen, it was really a race to Kinnaber as the first train cleared through the junction was the victor for that night.

Chapter 1

The Dawn of the Railway Age

'My fellow-passenger had the highest of all terrestrial qualities which for me a fellow-passenger can possess,' recalled Jane Carlyle, wife of the historian Thomas Carlyle. 'He was silent.'

Forget the Christmas card scene of a stagecoach carrying cheery, rosy-cheeked travellers, racing along a road amid snow-covered fields. The reality was rather different. Jane Carlyle was travelling by coach, and while able to afford the relative comfort of an inside seat, that meant that she had to face spending many hours, perhaps even a day or two, in accommodation that was small and cramped with her unchosen fellow passengers.

It is hard today to realize just how important an advance the railway was when it first appeared as a form of public transport, breaking out from its early existence in quarries. During the previous century, business had been transformed by the arrival of the canals, dramatically cutting the costs of moving bulky goods such as coal, but canals were slow and expensive to build, facing considerable problems when forced through steep hills or over deep valleys and always demanding the provision of large quantities of water. That the canal system slashed the costs of bulk commodities such as coal so dramatically only shows just how difficult and costly transport was before the eighteenth century. The railway was easier to build and to operate, and from the outset it was far faster than any form of transport then known to man.

The railways arrived on the scene at a time when few people made lengthy journeys, with most going no further than the nearest town. The Christmas card glamour of the long-distance stagecoach, or its rival the mail coach, first introduced in 1784, was in reality so harsh and bleak, as well as being expensive, that it was not to be undertaken lightly. In winter, coaches squelched through mud or could be overwhelmed by snow, or find bridges swept away by rivers in flood, while in summer the roads were baked hard and the coaches banged from one deep rut to another. Coaches could, and sometimes did, overturn or get blown off an exposed stretch of road. Competition on the busiest routes could see some wild driving, with more than one stagecoach smashed to matchwood in an accident. The arrival of the turnpike trusts in the early eighteenth century, due to much improved road-building and mending techniques, brought a considerable improvement, except that stretches of non-turnpike highway were still to be found between the turnpikes, themselves not wholly popular among those who had always used the roads free of any charge or taxation and who were damned if they were going to pay anything now, even for better roads.

Turnpike or not, passengers froze in winter despite heavy clothing, blankets and foot warmers, and sweltered in summer, longing for the next stop and liquid refreshment. Those outside fared worst, and even on a good road could not seek solace in sleep because to nod off was to fall off! Another consideration on any journey was one's fellow passengers, especially if travelling inside, for which privilege one paid double.

Meals were served at inns, and at many of them passengers were treated to rotten food badly prepared by unscrupulous proprietors, well aware that they had a captive market, anxious to absorb some sustenance in an all too brief halt – as little as twenty minutes – before being hurried back to their coach. Few people were regular travellers, so it was fair to assume that few of the customers would pass that way again. The hungry customers, perhaps on a journey taking as long as sixty hours, paid their money and were often cheated. Scalding hot soup would be served, so that customers with little time to eat, drink and doubtless perform other essential bodily functions as well, would not have time for subsequent courses. Food for these was, as a result, often stale. If one was contemplating a journey from, say, Edinburgh or Newcastle to London, it was worth considering going by sea, and coastal voyages were indeed an option. So too was travel by canal barge, on the relatively few routes served, which was slow but comfortable and relatively safe.

In the 1830s, at the dawn of the railway age, a passenger from London to Newcastle on the *Lord Wellington* coach would be charged £3 10s for the 274-mile journey, a fare of 3d per mile, for an outside seat. Ignoring inflation, this fare was exactly the same per mile as the standard rate for a second-class railway ticket in the early 1960s for a journey of up to 200 miles, after which the rate per mile fell. To put these fares into perspective, a footman in a grand house, by no means the most junior member of the servant class, would have been doing well to earn £20 per annum. Looked at another way, £3 10s in 1830 would be the equivalent of just over £200 today.

Assuming that you had decided to stay with the coach for the entire thirty-hour journey, in order to save money on accommodation along the way, what happened? Leaving London after lunch, your first chance of a break would be at Arrington Bridge for dinner, costing 2s 6d, while later you would be charged 3s at Huntingdon for sandwiches and cognac, the latter being an attempt to fight off the cold. There would have been other stops to change horses, but this was done in just two minutes. At Doncaster, breakfast awaited, provided that you had the necessary 2s 3d, but before you could get to your breakfast the guard, who would be changing, would expect a tip, usually around 2s 6d. Further on, at Ferrybridge, the driver would change and also expect a tip, another 2s. Lunch at York cost another 3s 6d, and the driver would be tipped again when he changed at Northallerton. Tea was taken at Rushyford Bridge, and cost just 2s. You reached Newcastle during the evening, no doubt exhausted, cramped, sore and cold. As you alighted you would be expected to tip both the guard and the driver, 2s 6d and 2s respectively. All in all, your £3 10s trip cost you £4 17s 3d, or more than £300 in today's money.

Drivers and guards were not backwards in seeking a tip: 'I'll be leaving you now sir ... your driver who has driven you the past fifty miles.'

All of this was for outside accommodation, exposed to the elements, dirt and dust. If you had opted to travel inside, your fare would have been £5 15s, and in addition to your meals, your driver and guard would have expected far higher tips, say 3s for the former and 3s 9d or even 4s for the latter.

All of these costs assume that your journey was a simple affair. If you lived in a village, or even in a small town, away from the main coaching routes, you would have had to make your way to the coach, and perhaps also make your own way to your destination at the end of the journey if that too was off the coaching map. This might mean walking, or perhaps hiring a carriage, at considerable additional expense.

Travelling north from London to Newcastle or Edinburgh, the traveller would have been spared one minor chore: changing the time on his or her watch. For those travelling east or west, it would have been wise to check the time whenever they stopped, as there was no conception of, and no need for, a single national time.

There is no doubt that the fares charged by the stagecoach operators were high, but the costs of providing this service, for up to six people inside and eleven outside on a stagecoach, with fewer outside on a mail coach as the seats at the back were reserved for the guard, were considerable, and the rewards were by no means guaranteed. On a run from London to Edinburgh, a single coach would need the services of 400 fine horses, with teams, usually of four, being changed in relays at the coaching inns.

Inevitably, Parliament soon saw an opportunity to raise money. Owners of carriages had been taxed as early as 1747, and their horses were taxed as well from 1785. As early as 1775, an annual duty was levied on each stagecoach of £5, followed in 1783 by a duty of a halfpenny for every mile run, doubled to 1d after a few years and then increased later, when a coach licensed to carry fifteen passengers could pay 3d per mile. There was also a tax on every coach and carriage produced that had to be paid by the carriage builders. Only mail coaches were exempt from taxation, on the grounds that they were employed on state business. On London to Edinburgh, the horses provided by contractors, usually at the inns along the way, would cost another £5, and the turnpikes would charge another £6 15s. Interestingly, travel by canal barge or shipment of goods by canal barge was free of taxation, although it had been proposed by William Pitt the Younger, who had wanted to tax the carriage of cargo in 1797, but backed down in the face of extremely strong opposition.

Given costs on such a scale for carrying so few people at speeds of around 12mph, it is not surprising that the new railway made an impact and that entrepreneurs could see that there was money to be made. At the beginning of the steam age, there were a number of attempts at harnessing steam to the stagecoach, but none were successful. Steam-powered carriages were heavy and damaged the roads, while the heavily rutted roads in turn produced such a rough ride that that mechanical reliability was seriously compromised. In any case, the costs continued to be high given the still small number of passengers that could be carried.

The Railways Arrive
Britain's railways were fragmented from the start. This was not a failure of organization or even a political decision, more the lack of it.

The government of the day did not decree that there should be lines linking London with this or that town or city, and perhaps later that there should be lines linking provincial cities. As one of only two countries – the other was the United States of America – to leave the development of the railways almost entirely to private enterprise, a means had to be found of raising money from investors. The funds required were so huge that this could only be done by offering digestible chunks of railway to the market.

A glance at the railway map in 1830 would have shown a series of lines widely separated and built with no intention of creating a network. This was not a failure of the private enterprise system; rather it was a sign of the times and of the parochial nature of planning, with the promoters of railway schemes thinking locally. Stockton needed to be linked with Darlington, Liverpool with Manchester, Canterbury with little Whitstable. At first, no one thought that there might be a need for a railway across the Pennines, or running from London to Scotland. One frequently overlooked advantage of this approach was that the United Kingdom saw cross-country routes developed as quickly and with as much enthusiasm as the trunk routes linking the provinces with London, in contrast to some European countries in which links between provincial centres were provided late and grudgingly at the taxpayers' expense.

While the first specific Parliamentary measures were the private bills designed to authorize the construction of railway lines, or other major works such as bridges and major termini, the first public bills did not follow for some time. This was not the practice on the Continent, with Belgium, for example, taking powers to control and direct the construction of railways as early as 1834. This could, of course, have been a reflection of the difference between the UK, 'where everything is permitted unless it is forbidden,' and those European countries, 'where everything is forbidden unless it is permitted.'

The government department responsible for the railways was the Board of Trade, and eventually this body decided that there should be a route linking London with Scotland. There was still no question of providing public money, but the promoters of the route would have the assurance of knowing that the enabling legislation would have government support. As a line had reached Lancaster, the Board favoured a line to Glasgow via Carlisle – what is now the West Coast Main Line – and this provoked a desperate attempt to create an East Coast route by one George Hudson, remembered as the 'Railway

King', who had successfully taken over the York and North Midland Railway and begun merging it with other companies. The trouble was that the North of England Railway was building a line from York to Newcastle, but by 1841 it had exhausted its capital and yet had only reached Darlington. It was left to Hudson to bring the various assorted railway interests involved in a line between York and Darlington to a meeting, from which he obtained their cooperation. His intervention was timely and the following year the necessary legislation passed through Parliament.

Not only new branch lines or extensions of main lines were built as small isolated projects, but so too were some of the London termini. At a time when the European Union demands that railways in member states should provide 'open access', it is worth reflecting that many of the new ventures floated during the nineteenth century assured would-be investors that their lines would be used by two or more railway companies. The extremely hard-up London Chatham & Dover Railway had succeeded in persuading both the Great Northern Railway and the London & South Western Railway to subscribe more than £300,000 apiece towards the cost of its lines to Blackfriars, then known as St Paul's, and the now-closed Ludgate Hill, with the promise of through running powers, which they soon exercised, along with the Midland Railway, which started running trains through to Victoria in 1875. The LCDR itself sent trains from Herne Hill through to King's Cross and then as far north as Barnet: this was a very useful Victorian north-south 'Thameslink' service, yet not a transport planner in sight!

It was also proof that fragmentation in itself was no obstacle to cooperation and through running. The arrangements made for different railways to have access to the better-placed London termini had their uses, but far more enduring arrangements saw through services from London to Scotland from Euston starting in 1858 and from King's Cross in 1862. This required cooperation on a grand scale, while there were the occasional outbreaks of competition between the operators of the East Coast and West Coast routes. Competition and cooperation became more intense when a third route from London to Scotland was opened in the mid-1870s by the Midland Railway, albeit on the longer route to both Edinburgh and Glasgow from St Pancras via Settle and Carlisle. The Midland did not offer speed, but it did offer comfort and was a very superior railway. Unlike the Great Western and the London Brighton & South Coast, two companies normally associated with having an up-market image, the Midland looked after its third-class passengers, and was the first company to provide third-class accommodation on all of its trains. Prior to the start of its Anglo-Scottish service the Midland made one of the single greatest advances ever in customer service by the simple expedient of abolishing its second-class fares and at the same time scrapping its third-class carriages, although, to put this into perspective, there were still relatively few of the latter. While it might have seemed more logical to have simply reduced the second-class fare to the third-class rate and scrapped the third-class carriages, thanks to Parliament third class was sacred, protected, and such a move was not allowed until many years after nationalization.

The operation of a service from Euston to Glasgow and Edinburgh required the London & North Western Railway to cooperate with the Caledonian Railway, while King's Cross to these cities required co-operation between the Great Northern, North Eastern and North British Railways, and for the passenger heading even further north to Aberdeen, the journey would have been over the lines of the Caledonian Railway. The Midland's partners on the Anglo-Scottish routes included the Glasgow & South Western and North British Railways. Given this thrust northwards and the rapid expansion of the railways, it is not surprising that, by 1848, the first signs of a network were evident on the railway maps. The opening of the Forth Bridge in 1890 made the East Coast line sixteen miles shorter than the West Coast for Aberdeen traffic and ended the advantage that the LNWR and Caledonian had hitherto enjoyed. Along the way, the traveller would pass through stations shared with other companies. The system worked, and endured until grouping in 1923.

Given the time taken to bring major infrastructure projects to fruition today, it is a salutary experience to look back on the expansion of the railway network. In 1844, there were already 2,236 route miles, but just six years later in 1850, this had grown to 6,084 miles, and then by almost half as much again to 9,069 miles in 1860. This rate of increase was maintained to reach 13,562 miles by 1870. By 1900, the mileage was 18,506 miles and still it continued to grow, not peaking until 1930 when there were 20,243 route miles, almost twice today's total mileage. The increase between 1900 and 1930 is all the more impressive because a number of lines were closed during the First World War, many of them never to reopen, to conserve fuel, manpower and equipment.

Of course, at first not everything on the railways marked a massive change from coaching practice. Those who have looked at illustrations of early railway carriages, or have visited museums, will have noticed that the early first-class carriages consisted of three stagecoach bodies joined together and mounted in tandem on a railway truck. It took a little time before designers explored the possibilities for the new mode of transport, and even then the preference for the first 100 years or so for compartment stock on Britain's railways can be traced back to stagecoach practice, while in the United States the open saloon was favoured from very early on. Another hangover from long-distance coach travel was that for many years longer-distance trains had to stop at stations to allow passengers to take food and drink, although this continuation of stagecoach practice was made even less desirable by the far larger numbers of people involved. The quality of the food on offer certainly did not improve.

> Until 1879, there were no dining-cars: hence the churning mobs who, like hopped-up dervishes, descended on station refreshment-stalls, hoping to snatch and gobble down a meal before their train steamed off again. Their enthusiasm tended to wane once they had sampled the food; scalding, discoloured water described as tea or coffee, greasy soup, dry buns and biscuits, and endless arrays of musty pork-pies that were almost museum pieces. Unfinished cups of coffee were poured back into the urn ready for the next batch of customers. (*Taken for a Ride*, Ivor Smullen, Herbert Jenkins, London 1968)

Especially on journeys into London, your travel would also have been interrupted by a stop, tantalisingly close to your destination, for tickets to be checked. It took some time before someone thought of checking tickets at the barriers of the London termini, while non-corridor rolling stock remained even on express trains on some lines as late as the 1920s, limiting the opportunities for on-board checks.

A rear-guard action was fought against improving the lot of the unfortunate traveller by the trade publication *Railway News*, which went to great lengths to prove that adding lavatories would put too much extra weight onto a train. There would also be the cost of providing towels, which *Railway News* was certain would be stolen by third-class passengers, and of plumbers to fill the roof cisterns. In the circumstances it is not surprising that, even into the twentieth century, travellers on many lines had to have strong bladders. The enlightened self-interest that would have improved facilities to enhance the appeal of railway travel was sadly lacking.

The Importance of the Mails

Mail traffic was so important that there were mail coaches as well as stagecoaches. As early as 1830, the Superintendent of Mail Coaches of the Post Office attended a board meeting of the Liverpool and Manchester Railway to discuss the basis on which mails could be conveyed between the two cities twice a day in each direction. This was forward-looking, and showed that the Post Office was not wed indefinitely to its own mail coach system, but was constantly looking for the fastest and most economical means of conveying the mails. In the case of the Liverpool and Manchester, agreement was reached that the mails would be carried for the princely sum of 2s 6d per thirty-mile trip. This seemingly insignificant start was to become an important source of railway revenues, and it was in many cases to have another impact on the railways, with certain express trains designated to carry mails. Often these were among the faster trains, even if timings owed more to the convenience of the Royal Mail than that of the passengers. Nothing much more happened until 1837 and the opening of the Grand Junction Railway, when once again an *ad hoc* arrangement was negotiated for mail between Birmingham and Liverpool, so that by using an overnight mail coach from London to Birmingham and then transferring to a morning train, Liverpool could be reached from London in sixteen and a half hours.

The Post Office was by now firmly convinced that the mail coaches were on the way out and that railways were here to stay, so the Railways (Conveyance of Mails) Act 1838 gave the Postmaster-General the power to require all railways, whether existing or proposed for the future, to carry the mail. The Act required the carriage of mail on both ordinary and special trains, and the latter were to operate at such times as the Post Office might direct. The measure also allowed for the mails to be carried in special rolling stock if the Post Office wished, for on-board sorting of mail in special carriages was already foreseen. Just as the stagecoaches transformed themselves during the period of transition from trunk carriers in their own right to feeders for the railways, the mail coaches also changed their role, filling in the gaps in the railway network, for there was absolutely no point in even attempting to compete with the all-conquering power of steam and wheel on rail.

The Post Office seems to have used the Act as a reserve measure, since by 1842, of the forty companies carrying mail, twenty-seven were doing so under notices issued under the Act, while the remainder had obviously concluded voluntary agreements with the Post Office. The Act allowed negotiation of the remuneration to be paid to the railway companies. It can only be supposed that those companies that had to be directed to carry the mails were those with unduly high expectations.

Taxation and Cheap Travel

Even before Parliament considered regulating the railways, it did what every administration throughout history has done: it considered taxing them! Taxation of railway travel began as early as 1832, when railways were so few and far between, and their routes so short, that it hardly seemed to matter. Railway companies were made to pay what was then the not insubstantial duty of ½d per mile for every four passengers carried, and the relative significance of the railways compared to stagecoach travel at this time can be judged by the fact that in 1835–37 the Treasury collected £13,000 annually from the railways against £750,000 (worth about £42 million today) from the stagecoach operators. As duties go, this 'passenger tax', as it became known, was a clumsy instrument since it made no distinction between the class of passenger, and so bore more heavily on the poorer passengers than the more affluent travelling in second or first class. It was not until 1844 that the first attempt was made to ease this situation.

By 1833, a growing body of opinion was concerned about the rapid expansion of the railway network, supported by an increasing volume of unrelated private bills with no overall shape or form. As concern rose, the House of Commons established not one but two committees to look into regulation of the railways, with the result being the recommendation from the second committee in 1838 that a new board be established to oversee the railways. It was suggested that this should be annexed to the Board of Trade. The result was the first Railway Regulation Act 1840, which established the Railway Department of the Board of Trade, and this was followed by a second measure in 1842. Some commentators have pointed out that the Board of Trade was ill-equipped for its new role, with no knowledge or understanding of the railways, but at the time how many people could claim to have this, outside the frantic world of the rapidly expanding railways? In fact the Board of Trade was already the repository of a certain amount of information on the railways, having been collecting statistics on the railways since 1832, and the statistician concerned, G.R. Porter, was put in charge of the new department and given a solicitor to help in the scrutiny of all railway legislation, including the private legislation empowering the construction of new lines and major works. All in all, the new Department had just five people in it, but then the entire Board of Trade at the time employed just thirty people. The initial powers of the Railway Department were the essential ones of ensuring that the railway companies provided returns on their traffic, that new lines were inspected before opening and that accidents were investigated. The inspectors were all officers in the Royal Engineers and so well suited to an assessment of the engineering, and especially civil engineering, aspects of the railways, but naturally enough completely ignorant about the operational and financial aspects. Even the knowledgeable Porter was, in 1845, concerned that the fledgling railways would not be able to compete with the arrival of steam boats on the River Thames. He need not have worried.

In addition to awarding powers to the Board of Trade, the 1840 Act also provided for the punishment of 'railway servants' for safety transgressions. Such legislation was necessary because the Board of Trade almost seems to have acquired its responsibilities for the railways by default rather than by design, and there was to be no such thing as a Ministry of Transport until after the First World War. The Board of Trade had originally developed to oversee the country's overseas trade and through this assumed responsibility for shipping. In its original form, the Board of Trade was not concerned with the inland transport of the United Kingdom, and indeed was none too concerned about domestic trading arrangements.

Nevertheless, it now became apparent that there was much to be done to correct and control the growth of the railways. The European system of central direction was considered, and Gladstone, as President of the Board of Trade, was especially keen to overhaul the system. No doubt much of this was necessary, but it was inevitable even then that an ambitious politician would be keen to extend the powers of his department.

The famous railway entrepreneur George Hudson's representations to the committee chaired by Gladstone early in 1844 are mentioned later. Gladstone had by this time been an MP since 1832, but more significantly he was probably one of the better-informed members as far as railways were concerned, since his father, Sir John, had been an enthusiastic promoter of the early railways in Scotland, and by 1843 had accumulated £170,000 (around £10 million today) of railway investments. The only real question was how impartial his son could be. On the one hand, it could account for the watering down of the early provisions of the Railway Bill that resulted from the committee's deliberations, but on the other, shortly after the measure was enacted, Gladstone resigned, largely because he was aware of the conflict of interest between his own family's involvement in railways and his powers as their Parliamentary overlord. He maintained this distance between himself and railway regulation for the remainder of his life, attending only two sessions of Cardwell's Committee on Railways, which sat in 1852–53, even though he was nominally a member, and avoiding service altogether on the 1865 Royal Commission on Railways. However, in later life Gladstone did not maintain a physical distance between himself and the railway, as he was the only prominent British politician to use the railways during electioneering, often addressing crowds at railway stations and even from carriage windows, a style more usually associated with the United States than the United Kingdom, probably because at the time it was still a practical proposition for an individual to hire a train.

The Railway Regulation Act 1844 has become more commonly known as 'Gladstone's Act'. The most significant provisions were for cheap railway travel, a predecessor of the later 'Cheap Trains Act', while telegraph companies were enabled to compel railway companies to allow their wires to be carried alongside their lines and, for the first time, the possibility of nationalization of the railways was enshrined in British law. Gladstone himself felt that the Act had been an opportunity missed, and that the powers contained within the Act were far too weak, largely due to the power of the railway companies, who had many members of both Houses of Parliament among their shareholders and directors.

The importance of the Act should not be underestimated, as it authorized the purchase of railway companies by a British government in the future, although it applied only to those companies established after 1 January 1845, and the powers could not be exercised before 1866. The price to the government of a railway company was to be the profits for a twenty-five-year period, averaged out over the preceding three years. As we shall see, by the mid-1860s many railway companies were passing through a bleak period and no doubt the cost of acquisition at the time would have been low, but the railway system was still incomplete. One cannot help wonder, had nationalization occurred at this early stage, whether the total mileage would ever have reached its ultimate grand total of more than 20,000 miles? Given post-nationalization experience of the attitude of the Treasury to investment in the railways, one may be excused for doubting it.

Cheap Travel for All

The cheap travel provisions of the 1844 Act created what came to be known as 'Parliamentary Trains', establishing certain standards of speed and comfort for these while carrying passengers at very low fares. This combination owed its origins to an accident on Christmas Eve 1841, when a Great Western train was derailed at Sonning, just to the east of Reading, killing eight third-class passengers who had been travelling in a goods train's low-sided open wagons. In the ensuing inquiry, the inspector pointed out the dangers of travelling in such unsuitable accommodation. This provoked a general investigation by the Railway Department into the provision made for third-class passengers throughout the country, and it was found that the GWR example was more the rule than the exception. Many trains had no provision at all for third-class passengers. As a result, the 1844 Act stipulated that all future railways defined as passenger railways, meaning that they earned a third or more of their turnover from passenger fares, would have to provide at least one daily train, including Sundays, that would call at every station and have an overall speed, allowing for stops, of not less than 12mph, and that the passengers would have to be carried in enclosed carriages provided with seats. It was also stipulated that the fares would not exceed 1d per mile, and for this each passenger would be entitled to carry up to 56lb (25.4kg) of luggage, rather more than economy-class airline passengers are allowed, and much more than the 33lb (15kg) of many charter flights. To help the railways provide this basic service, these low fares were exempted from passenger tax, by this time at a rate of five per cent, which of course meant that it no longer weighed most heavily on the poorer passengers. On some railways, this became the new third class, while others provided both Parliamentary trains and third-class trains, although strictly speaking third-class fares were still subject to passenger tax.

The new measure was only enforceable on future railways, but most of the railway companies complied with it anyway. This was not simply a gesture of goodwill. The way in which new lines and extensions to existing lines were sanctioned by private acts of Parliament meant that any other arrangement would have been cumbersome and impractical. Indeed, there is considerable evidence, especially in

Scotland, that many railways bitterly objected to the new measure on the grounds that many passengers who could afford much more were travelling in the Parliamentary trains and thus depriving them, and of course the Treasury, of revenue. In another sense, the new measure was itself scarcely a model of common sense, doubtless because the Treasury was anxious to see as few passengers as possible escape paying tax. An ordinary third-class passenger, possibly commuting, although the term was unknown at the time, to a place of employment, was taxed regardless of his or her circumstances. Then too, while the 12mph speed was good for a stopping train in 1844, this later became slow and unattractive, but a subsequent court decision in 1874 ruled that a train that did not stop at every station along its route could not be classed as a 'Parliamentary' train and had to pay the tax.

Even so, the generosity of Parliament was not always appreciated by those who used the trains. In 1883, F.S. Williams wrote in *Our Iron Roads*:

> To start in the darkness of a winter's morning to catch the only third-class train that ran; to sit, after a slender breakfast, in a vehicle the windows of which were compounded of the largest amount of wood and the smallest amount of glass, carefully adjusted to exactly those positions in which the fewest passengers could see out; to stop at every roadside station, however insignificant; and to accomplish a journey of 200 miles in about ten hours – such were the ordinary conditions which Parliament in its bounty provided for the people.

The Railway Entrepreneur

Imagine, if you will, that a former British prime minister has a sister who has invested heavily in a company, one which is active in exploiting a new technology, but she has been seriously embarrassed by a massive fall in the value of her shares. Still a prominent figure, the prime minister discusses the problem with a leading industrialist, known and respected for his experience in the new technology. The industrialist solves the problem by investing in the company in question and making his investment known. So high is his reputation, that other investors hastily follow the great man and invest, so that the share price rises, at which point the prime minister's sister sells her shares and, doubtless with a huge sigh of relief, banks the cash. No doubt the industrialist does the same, for although he may have been doing a good deed for an important and influential friend, he himself is not a charity.

This would be construed as rigging the share price. Scandalous, is it not? How would the press and Parliament react today?

In fact, the former prime minister in question was none other than the Duke of Wellington, the victor at Waterloo and throughout his lifetime a national hero, while the industrialist was the so-called 'Railway King', the Yorkshireman George Hudson.

Neither gentleman comes out well in this little episode, but who would you suggest was the more blameworthy, Wellington or Hudson? I would suggest the former, as a prime minister should be above such behaviour. Yet history has generally been kind to Wellington, rightly a national hero, but far less kind to Hudson, so often portrayed as a villain. Of course, one might suggest that Wellington didn't know how things ought to be done, having been a bluff soldier for so much of his life. That might be true. Certainly, after his first cabinet meeting on becoming prime minister, he remarked what an odd experience it had been, since he had given them their orders and then they had wished to stay and discuss them! On the other hand, Hudson also did much that would be frowned upon today, so perhaps we are making the mistake of judging the actions of those in the past by modern standards. That is always a serious error and one that, if it does not actually rewrite history, certainly interferes with a true understanding of it.

The railway age did not simply improve communications and provide for the first time a single standard time across the British Isles. (The railways brought the need for a single standard national time, or 'railway time', which became the direct predecessor of Greenwich Mean Time.) It did not even simply allow people to move out from overcrowded slums and into less crowded and more congenial dormitory towns or the rapidly expanding suburbs, termed the 'Metroland' effect. The impact of the railways was far more pervasive than this, for they materially affected the way in which business functioned in its most basic sense, the raising of capital. While this was happening, the railways also dramatically increased the extent to which Parliament felt it could, and indeed should and would, intervene in business activity. Because the railways were often seen as having a monopoly, at least locally, despite the multitude of companies, some compared the iron road with the public highway, especially when at first many railways were meant to be open to anyone who wanted to run a train. Thus the railways also brought into being the concept of nationalization, of state ownership, even though the first example of this was in another form of communications altogether, the telegraph system. The railways marked the change from the state providing a service, such as the Royal Mail, to the takeover of a functioning business, or businesses.

The railways were also one of the prime movers in the way businesses were structured. In a modern business, the liability of investors is limited to their investment in the business. No one is going to pursue them until all of the creditors have been paid, unlike in a partnership, where if the partners cannot meet their share of the liabilities and declare themselves bankrupt, the creditors may continue to press for payment from any remaining partners who still may have assets. The loss of an investment is no small thing, but it is reassuring if the liability stops at that. This concept of limited liability, of the joint stock company, was brought about by another piece of legislation, the Joint Stock Companies Act 1862, which encouraged the investment to fund the continued expansion of the railways. Thanks to the railways, the stock markets and the exchanges (for most large cities, such as Bristol, had their own stock exchanges at this time) that served them developed alongside the railways, which were not simply hungry for capital, but were devouring it at an unprecedented rate. No one had ever seen such massive enterprises, with their demand for large tracts of land, needing not only track and signals, locomotives and carriages or goods wagons, but also stations, engine sheds, even their own locomotive and carriage-building facilities, as well as massive bridges and viaducts.

Despite this, railways could bring bankruptcy, but they could also bring prosperity. York was jealous of the impact of the industrial revolution on Leeds and Bradford, but itself retained its earlier prosperity, built on the city being at the heart of an agricultural area, by becoming a railway city. Otherwise it might have remained something of a backwater, as in the case of, to take another great cathedral city as an example, Lincoln. It is simply little short of miraculous that York retained all of its beauty and dignity despite becoming a great railway city with workshops and a major station, itself contributing to the city's architectural glory. No other railway city can have been so important yet so unspoiled.

The Railway King

The story of no one man quite encapsulates the rollercoaster ride that was the lot of the early railway entrepreneur than that of George Hudson who, at the peak of his powers, was the chairman of four railway companies covering a wide geographical spread. By 1850 he controlled a quarter of the nation's railway route mileage, then over 6,000 miles, itself probably equalling the total route mileage in the rest of the world at the time. Hudson managed his empire, which included docks and property interests as well as railways, without a telephone, fax, e-mail, typewriters, calculating machines or computers, and without a massive head office. Perhaps the absence of these 'essential' tools of modern management held the key to his success.

The modern manager works within two frameworks. One is the regulatory framework that has grown up over the years, and the other is the network of specialists with which he is surrounded. The only specialist for George Hudson was the great railway engineer George Stephenson, for he was a civil engineer as well as a mechanical engineer, and doubtless much else as well. Combining the different engineering roles would not be possible today, but it did mean that problems were seen in the round rather than in isolation.

George Hudson was no business school graduate. He was from a farming family and was born in 1800 in the small Yorkshire village of Howsham, which he left under a cloud at the tender age of fifteen years after fathering an illegitimate child by a local girl. He made his way to York, where he worked in a draper's shop, marrying the owner's daughter and later, in 1827, receiving the then considerable inheritance of £30,000 (about £1.5 million today), from a distant relative.

Hudson was later to say that the inheritance was the worst thing that could have happened to him. It enabled him to become active in local politics, becoming Mayor of York three times, and also to invest in local railway schemes. In 1836 he was elected chairman of the York & North Midland Railway, which linked his adopted city with London, albeit by a circuitous route via Derby and Rugby, taking 217 miles, but nevertheless offering four through trains a day, with the journey from York to London taking ten hours compared with around twenty hours by stagecoach. The company leased and then later absorbed adjoining lines, as well as building a number of extensions itself. The York & North Midland Railway from the outset seemed to be prosperous and, as mentioned earlier, Hudson pressed for a major trunk route up the East Coast to Scotland. This was a more difficult ambition to realize. Part of the problem was that the line being built by the North of England Railway from York to Newcastle was in serious difficulties, and by 1841 it had exhausted its capital and only managed to reach as far north as Darlington. The directors had no option but to open the forty-five miles between York and Darlington to generate some income, something that should have been planned from the outset. The route between York and Darlington had been easy to build, but further north the terrain became more difficult, while the line was crossed by a number of smaller companies, including the pioneering Stockton & Darlington, who were alarmed by the arrival of the larger and more ambitious newcomer. Hudson was dismayed by this situation, as not only was his vision of a line to Newcastle and beyond compromised, but the Board of Trade had finally started to take an interest in creating strategic routes. Wanting to link London with Scotland, they had opted for a route from Carlisle to Edinburgh using a competing route that had already reached as far north as Lancaster. It was left to Hudson to bring the various railway interests involved in a line between York and Darlington to a meeting, from which he obtained their cooperation.

All Hudson now had to do was finance the scheme, but the £500,000 (around £30 million today) needed was, Hudson felt, unlikely to be raised on the open market, so he suggested that each of the companies present should offer shares in the proposed line to their own shareholders, almost what would today be described as a rights issue, with a guaranteed dividend of six per cent. A new company was formed, the Newcastle & Darlington Junction Railway, with Hudson, of course, as chairman. It was not until 1842 that the necessary legislation was passed through Parliament, and the difficulty of the process and its importance was undoubtedly a factor in Hudson deciding to become an MP.

Meanwhile, the York & North Midland had been doing well, paying a ten per cent dividend at a time of recession, but the North Midland, over which much of its traffic proceeded, was suffering. Hudson headed a committee enquiring into the affairs of this company, and within a week proposed a dramatic reduction in expenses, cutting these from £44,000 weekly to £27,000 through a combination of redundancies and reducing wages, as well as looking for economies elsewhere. This decisive action saved the company, but its neighbours, the Midland Counties and the Birmingham & Derby Junction, were also suffering difficulties, having been built during a boom and by this time involved in ruinous competition with each other. With remarkable clarity of purpose, Hudson proposed a merger of all three companies, one that would achieve still further savings, with the new Midland Railway formed in September 1843, with the then considerable capital of £5 million (£300 million today).

This was the height of the railway mania that was gripping the country. Speculators and small investors with their hard-earned savings alike headed into the new railway stocks, and Parliament was in danger of being swamped by the tidal wave of private bills, each of which was intended to authorize a railway, often only for short stretches of line. Some were links in a grander and more ambitious scheme, some satisfied a local need, some seemed to be a whim. It was this almost as much as the Sonning accident on the Great Western that had sparked the 1844 legislation mentioned earlier. Gladstone planned to regulate the railways 'for the public benefit.' Hudson appeared before the Commons select committee, and forecast that the railway bubble was about to burst and that many of the new and proposed lines would turn out to be unviable, although he staunchly maintained that '... the public would rather (the railways) be in the hands of companies than ... government.'

Nevertheless, Gladstone's bill, when published, foresaw a form of state control, and Hudson was asked by the directors of the other railway companies to head resistance to the measure. Thus, when the Parliamentary process was complete, the Railway Act 1844 saw most of the troublesome and unwelcome clauses of the original bill omitted.

On 18 June 1844, the thirty-nine miles of the Newcastle & Darlington Junction Railway opened. The railway journey from York to London had taken ten hours in 1837, but by 1844 the much longer journey from Gateshead to London took just eight hours, a clear indication of progress. The next step was for Hudson's friend and colleague George Stephenson to build a bridge across the Tyne, while two separate companies were promoted, in true railway expansion fashion, with one for the line between Newcastle and Berwick-on-Tweed, and the other to link Berwick with Edinburgh. Later, Hudson was to consolidate his position at Newcastle by taking control of the line from Newcastle to Carlisle, and from Carlisle to Maryport.

Hudson became Conservative MP for Sunderland in 1845, largely because his railway ambitions could be helped by a seat in the House of Commons. While he did much to improve the town's docks, he was also driven by a desire to sabotage the plans for a direct line between York and London, which later became the Great Northern Railway, and in 1846 this drew him into taking over the Eastern Counties Railway, which was struggling financially and also failing to provide a safe service. This was not a disinterested move by Hudson, for he saw the Eastern Counties line from London to Cambridge as the first link in a feasible alternative to the Great Northern route to York. The route via Cambridge would, he estimated, cost £4 million, but that was just half the estimated cost of the Great Northern route. Hudson won over the Eastern Counties shareholders by trebling dividends and, although operations improved under Hudson's stewardship, it soon became clear that he was paying dividends out of capital. This was unacceptable, but a fairly commonplace practice at the time. In 1849, an inquiry found that no less than £200,000 (£15 million today) had been paid out in this way. This raised questions among those concerned with his other companies, and it was soon found that the same practice was being applied, so by the end of 1849 he was forced to resign all of his chairmanships. By this time, the Great Northern route was open and, pragmatic to the end, Hudson decided to use the new route and abandon his own plans to extend the Eastern Counties line, with the result that he came under pressure from angry Midland Railway shareholders who objected to the diversion of traffic away from their route and on to the more direct route.

Had the railway boom continued, Hudson could have avoided the problems that beset him over paying dividends out of capital. His ruse would have been disguised as money continued to flood in from enthusiastic investors, while the seemingly insatiable appetite for railway travel on the most suitable lines would have seen revenues develop to the stage where his misuse of capital would no longer be necessary. It was not to be. Claim after claim was lodged against Hudson, who continued to the end to attract warm local support in both Sunderland and Whitby, as the inhabitants of both towns saw him as a local benefactor. Initially, Hudson was able to fight off the threat of bankruptcy by selling his extensive estates, which he had acquired to leave to his sons, and afterwards because as a sitting MP he could not be arrested for bankruptcy. When he lost his Parliamentary seat, he was forced to flee to France, and spent many years in and out of exile. He was rescued in the end by legislation ending imprisonment of debtors, and by an annuity from capital raised by his friends.

Opinions of Hudson differ, and no more spirited and credible defence has been raised on his behalf than in *The Railway King* by Robert Beaumont. It is true that he committed fraud by paying dividends out of capital, and in some cases sold shares between his companies at an inflated price. Using capital to pay dividends was not uncommon at the time, and, faced with the need to keep fickle investors on board long enough to complete projects, many succumbed to this temptation, which could escape notice if all went well. The concept of an independent auditor was unknown at the time, although no doubt Hudson's manoeuvrings expedited its adoption.

Conversely, Hudson was a man of whom it could be said that he got things done, and he provided well-paid jobs for many thousands of workers, as well as creating many miles of much-needed railway line. Indeed, his feeding traffic onto the rival Great Northern route was in recognition of the basic fact that traffic would follow the quickest and most direct route, so better by far to cooperate than to compete to the discomfort and inconvenience of passengers. Hudson also had many rivals, some of whose methods and motives were suspect, but in contrast to Hudson, many of them, such as George Leeman, the York solicitor, were also hypocritical. There can be no doubt that many anxious and greedy investors benefited from his behaviour, including a number in high places, and when faced with his difficulties, he could have eased the pressure on himself by naming names, or perhaps paid his way out of his own debts by calling in debts owed to him, or even blackmailing those who had done well by him. He did none of these things. In the end, he even came to arrangements with his remaining creditors and was considering a return to Parliament when he died suddenly in 1871.

The spirit of the age was that many entrepreneurs saw investors' money almost as their own, and if they were doing something for the benefit of the company, they felt free to use it at will. While stock market and accountancy regulations were at an early stage, Hudson was not the first, and certainly not the last, to feel that the end justified the means. However, while amassing what was at one stage a great fortune for himself and for his heirs, all of which was lost, he did not rob people. Everyone felt that they should share in this boom, no one saw the dangers, and the pressure was on. The country in return gained a massive railway network without public expense, so much so that during the Second World War, even though on occasions the London termini were closed by bombing, routes created in the days of competition were always available between London and the Midlands and the Channel coast. Today, despite the UK having only forty-four per cent of the land area of France, it still has seven per cent more railway miles, even after the closure of half the system, and twenty-four per cent more railway than Japan, despite that country being fifty-four per cent larger.

Chapter 2

A Tale of Four Cities

At the start of the railway age, many of our largest cities were already sizeable. Birmingham was fast becoming the 'workshop of the world' and Glasgow liked to vie with Birmingham for the position of being the second largest city in the British Empire, still itself far from its peak, which was not reached until after the First World War.

This book is really about the railways linking London with Edinburgh and Glasgow, and then with Aberdeen. All four cities have changed in the century and more since the railways began to race. London had a strong industrial base at the time and was not over-preoccupied with politics and finance as it is today, and much the same can be said of Edinburgh, although it was already a 'well set up' city at the time, it was not yet the draw for tourists it is today. Glasgow was one of the world's most prominent centres for shipbuilding, if not *the* most important, and both Glasgow and its rival, Edinburgh, had extensive coal-mining districts within easy reach of the city centre. Aberdeen had fish and the agricultural produce of the rich farmlands of Grampian, but in those far-off days before the advent of the internal combustion engine no one imagined the boom that North Sea oil would bring.

Perhaps the only thing that all four cities had in common was a water frontage, although some in Edinburgh would argue that Leith, the Scottish capital's port area, was a separate entity. Only Aberdeen was actually on the sea, squeezed between the outfalls of the rivers Dee and Don, although Edinburgh, or to be more precise Leith, was at least on the tidal waters of the Firth of Forth. Glasgow sat on the Clyde and London on the Thames, but Edinburgh's river, the Water of Leith, was, and is, more of a stream and is not navigable.

London

No mode of transport could ignore London. The River Thames had ensured the capital's value as a port and, while it might be an exaggeration to say that all roads led to London, it was nevertheless both the start and the end of a network of major highways, as the Romans had chosen it as the lowest place at which they could bridge the Thames. When the canals had arrived, and proved just as significant a step forward in reducing transport costs and improving communications as the railways were to be later, London was on the canal network. The most obvious of these was the Grand Union Canal, linking London with Birmingham, but there were others linking into the docks, then much further upstream than is the case today. For the canal users, the Regent's Canal, completed as late as 1820 and curving around the northern and already heavily built-up suburbs, was a vital link around London, but for the railways, it was another obstacle to be overcome.

Despite the earliest railways being built away from London and between pairs of towns with local trading interests, it was inevitable that lines would be sent into London at an early date. London presented both opportunities and problems for those entrepreneurs anxious to develop the railways. The opportunities included its size and the congestion, the fact that it was a political, legal and financial capital, the largest port, and that it needed fresh food and coal brought to it in vast quantities. The problems were the congestion and the sheer impossibility of fitting anything easily into this dense mass of humanity, housing and industry, as well as the poor drainage, especially south of the River Thames, while to the north, once clear of the centre, there were hills, the 'northern heights', and gradients to overcome.

London's first railway was the Surrey Iron Railway, a horse-drawn tramroad built to carry freight from the Thames, and authorized by Parliament in 1801. The capital's first steam-driven railway, the London & Greenwich Railway, was authorized in 1833. Raising the necessary capital proved difficult at first and so, like many lines, it opened in stages between early 1836 and late 1838, despite being just three and a half miles in length.

In driving through the better-class areas from the north-west, the London & Birmingham not only had landowners to deal with, but also residents who had a voice and a pen, and knew how to use them. The inhabitants of these areas may well have been renting their properties, but they were a class apart from those affected by the first London railways. Today, with widespread property ownership, it is easy to forget that in pre-Victorian Britain, and even during the Victorian period, home ownership was very much in the minority, even among the upper middle and professional classes.

The London & Birmingham was checked on the outskirts and settled at Euston Square which, once the underground railways arrived, proved not to be the most convenient location. While it eventually had its own station on the Hampstead Tube, now the Northern Line, it was not so well-sited for the Circle and Metropolitan lines, at least not for the passenger with heavy luggage to carry.

It is only with hindsight that we can assess the efforts of the early railway planners. The Great Western wanted to keep costs to a minimum and share Euston with the London & Birmingham. Nevertheless, the ambitions and suspicions of the backers of the railways got in the way and negotiations broke down, forcing the GWR to build its own terminus at Paddington and leaving the London & Birmingham alone at Euston. As both the original termini soon proved too small and had to be expanded, it was a blessing that they were not forced to share the same terminus. In any case, part of the problem at Euston, and some of the other London termini such as King's Cross, was on the approaches, and this remains the case. These mighty stations have approaches which are literally 'choke' points.

Euston opened in 1837. William Hardwick was commissioned as Euston's architect and the approach to the station portrayed its greatness with a magnificent Doric portico. People travelled to view the new station, which seemed to say so much about what was to become known variously as the 'steam age' and the 'Victorian era', and boded so well for both. It got even better, for by 1849 Euston had acquired a Great Hall and a Shareholders' Room. On the other hand, the train shed that lay beyond this grandeur was a disappointment, for low iron fabrications covered the two platforms, and there was no question that cheapness awaited the traveller after he had purchased his ticket.

The early railway termini differed greatly from those of today, having separate arrival and departure platforms. Even as they grew, this system prevailed for many years. Illogical to modern eyes, these spoke of a more leisurely age when a train would arrive, and its carriages would be taken away for cleaning after the passengers had alighted, while the locomotive would reverse and 'run light', in railway parlance, to an engine shed to receive water and coal. This system eventually came under scrutiny because of the amount of space required for running roads for carriage workings and locomotive workings, but the death knell really came with the arrival of first electric and then diesel traction. This meant that trains could be driven into the terminus, then while the passengers alighted and the train waited for fresh passengers to board, the driver simply walked from a cab at one end of the train to one at the other. Even when diesel locomotives or electric engines were used, a replacement was simply coupled on to the other end of the train, or in railway parlance the 'rake' of passenger carriages, ready to take it on its return journey, leaving that which had worked the train into the terminus to reverse out into a siding, and await its turn to take the next departure. Many of the early stations, even those which are today major termini, would have just one or two arrival platforms and a single departure platform.

At this stage, railway travel was still in its infancy. A dozen departures a day would be commonplace, far less than in even an off-peak hour at a major terminus today.

The famous Great Exhibition of 1851 was a defining moment in the history of transport in London. The concept of exhibitions really dates from the Victorian era and the Great Exhibition, for which the Crystal Palace was built in London's Hyde Park, was simply the grandest and most famous of them. Such exhibitions were not possible before the railway age, as no means existed of moving so many people, or the exhibits themselves. In an age that still knew few public holidays, the excursion trains to the Great Exhibition were the first mass holiday travel. The nearest thing to this before the Great Exhibition had been the more popular racing events.

The ability to convey large exhibits more economically and efficiently than any other mode of transport also came into play with the Great Exhibition, and indeed the exhibits included two steam locomotives. Open from 1 May to 15 October 1851, the Great Exhibition saw six million tickets sold. While the site did not have a railway connection and many arrived on foot, the business generated for the railways was considerable. It also boosted other businesses as well, with Thomas Cook, founder of the eponymous travel agency, becoming the Midland Railway's agent for the Great Exhibition in London, for which he provided tickets and other arrangements for 165,000 people.

For the railways the exhibition showed that many of the existing arrangements were far from suitable. On the Great Northern Railway, the London terminus at King's Cross had still to be built, but the temporary station at Maiden Lane was named 'King's Cross' in the timetable, even though it consisted of just two timber platforms, which had to cope with the traffic of 1851 and were also by Queen Victoria and Prince Albert for their trip to Scotland that August.

Eventually King's Cross was built, but the line had to be buried under the Regent's Canal and then pass through the 528-yard Gas Works tunnel. The 'real' King's Cross was built on a ten-acre site which had been occupied by the Small Pox and Fever Hospitals, while a number of houses were also demolished. It opened on 14 October 1852. Initially, the daily service consisted of twelve trains in each direction, with just three of them expresses, with departures starting at 7.00am and ending at 8.00pm, while the last arrival was at 10.00pm. Passengers were met by horse buses, which for 6d would convey them to London Bridge, Waterloo or Paddington.

Lewis Cubitt designed a simple yet practical station, with two 800ft-long, 105ft-wide train sheds, which were joined at the southern end by a 216ft façade of London stock bricks with two arches, but with little ornament. The lack of pretension was spoiled somewhat by a central square clock tower, 112ft high, with an Italianate turret and a clock with three faces (the north-facing one was blocked off as it could not be seen from the ground). The clock's chimes were silenced at the outbreak of the First World War and not reinstated until 1924, then silenced again in 1927. The west side of the station had a departure platform, now No. 10, while on the east was an arrival platform, now No. 1, with fourteen carriage roads in between them. A carriage road ran alongside the arrival platform, while between the departure platform and an external carriage road were refreshment rooms and first- and second-class waiting rooms and ladies' rooms, as well as the station offices. As was the custom at the time, a hotel was also built, opening in 1854, but the Great Northern Hotel was set apart from the station to the south-west.

Around three-quarters of the roof was glazed, supported by arches and laminated wood girders, which had to be replaced on the east side during 1869–70, and on the west during 1886–87.

Once finished, King's Cross was the largest terminus in the British Isles, and the GNR was accused of extravagance. This was denied by the Board, who pointed out that they had obtained good value. In fact, the portico and Grand Hall at Euston had cost as much.

At the start, King's Cross was a mainline station, with just four stations between London and Hatfield, some seventeen and three-quarter miles away, but intermediate stations were opened over the next decade or so. In February 1858, the GNR trains were joined by those of the Midland Railway, although these were later removed when St Pancras was opened in September 1868. Shortly after the Metropolitan Railway opened in 1863, a station was opened at King's Cross slightly to the east of the terminus, and in October of that year all GNR suburban trains were diverted to Farringdon Street, with up suburban trains having to back into the terminus, using the departure platform: up trains had to stop at a platform outside the terminus named York Road, before descending to the Metropolitan.

Further massive disruption and demolition of housing was required for St Pancras when it was built for the Midland Railway's extension to London after the original arrangement, which saw trains running from Hitchin to King's Cross starting in early 1858, had proved expensive. The heavy excursion traffic for the Great Exhibition of 1851 also showed the limitations on capacity at King's Cross, even before the growth in the Great Northern Railway's traffic in the years that followed. It was clear the MR needed its own terminus and its own approach route.

The MR already had its own goods yard in London at Agar Town, between the North London Railway and the Regent's Canal. It was decided to extend this line to the Euston Road, at the boundary set by the Royal Commission on London's Termini, which effectively barred further incursions by railways into the centre of London. A four and a half acre site was found for the terminus. The extension required the demolition of thousands of slum dwellings in Agar Town and Somers Town. In addition, the line to the terminus itself had to pass over the Regent's Canal, which meant both a falling gradient towards the terminus and a platform level some twenty feet above street level.

Initially, when William Barlow designed the station, he proposed filling the space under the tracks and platforms with soil excavated from the tunnels, but James Allport, the MR's general manager, saw the potential for storage space, especially for beer from Burton-on-Trent. This led Barlow to design a single-span trainshed, which not only allowed greater freedom in planning the storage space beneath the station, but also meant that the layout of the tracks and platforms could be altered as needed in the years to come. A large Gothic hotel was constructed in front of the station, giving it the most impressive frontage of any London terminus. While trains from Bedford to Moorgate started using the tunnel under the terminus from 13 July 1868, the terminus itself was opened to traffic on 1 October 1868, without any ceremony.

The Midland Grand Hotel was still at foundation level when the station opened, but this was intended to be the most luxurious of its kind, and a monument to its architect, Sir Gilbert Scott.

The station was meant to serve the MR's long-distance ambitions. The company saw its main market as the East Midlands, but while that was the basis of its traffic, its services to Scotland, which started in the 1870s, were also important. Despite having a local platform, there was almost no suburban traffic for many years, with the MR's suburban trains, never plentiful, working through to Moorgate. Even in 1903, there were just fourteen suburban arrivals between 5.00am and 10.00am. It was not until 1910 that the Midland Railway began to encourage suburban traffic at St Pancras.

Aberdeen

Prior to the advent of the railway, Aberdeen was isolated and the most reliable means of transport was by sea. Such was the enthusiasm for the new mode of transport that the Harbour Board made a site available close to the centre of the city for a terminus. While a prospectus was issued for the Aberdeen Railway as early as 1844, proposing a link with the Northern Junction Railway at Forfar, difficulties in construction, with a viaduct collapsing and a bridge being swept away in a flood, as well as the financial crisis of 1848, meant that the line did not open until 1850.

Meanwhile, the Great North of Scotland Railway approached the city from the north, using much of the route of the Aberdeen Canal, which was abruptly drained for the purpose. The GNSR did not share the Guild Street terminus of the AR, but instead stopped at Waterloo Quay, one and half miles away. It was not until 1867 that a connecting line through the Denburn Valley was completed and a joint station opened. This was replaced in 1915 by the present station, completed in sandstone.

The opening of the railway benefited both the fishing industry and agriculture, with Aberdeenshire farmers specializing in cattle fattening. Instead of sending live cattle by sea, butchered meat could be sent south by rail. Initially the city was reached from the south by the West Coast route, but after the completion of the bridges over the Forth and Tay, overnight fish and meat trains could reach the London markets at Billingsgate and Smithfield. A small network of commuter services was also established around Aberdeen, with workmen's trains to the Stoneywood paperworks by 1870, and later a suburban service linking

the city with Dyce, so that by the turn of a century, two million passengers a year were being carried. Nevertheless, these were short-
distance passengers and stations were close together, with eight in the
six miles to Dyce, so the service was vulnerable when motorbus competition appeared after the First World War. The suburban service
ended in 1937.

Edinburgh

Scotland's capital was already a tightly built up area by the time the
railways arrived, while the topography included high ridges running
from east to west. There was substantial passenger traffic to be had
from the affluent areas around the city centre, but goods traffic
depended on being able to reach the port and industrial area of Leith
to the north, and the coal-mining areas to the south. The first railway
was the horse-drawn Edinburgh & Dalkeith, which was extended to
the docks at Leith, but which was effectively a tramroad. When the
first steam railway, the Edinburgh & Glasgow, reached the city, it
stopped in the West End, a largely residential area then under construction, at Haymarket, with strong local opposition to any further
advance eastwards, and it was not until the North British Railway
arrived in 1846 that a short connecting line was built under the shadow
of the Castle to a new joint station at Waverley, situated out of sight in
a valley that divided the medieval Old Town from the Georgian New
Town. The Edinburgh Leith & Granton Railway, next to be built, had
its platforms at right angles to those of the NBR at Waverley and ran in
a tunnel under the New Town. The tunnel for the line has been closed
off, but can still be seen from near the station offices and is clearly
signed.

   History repeated itself in 1848 when the Caledonian Railway
reached Edinburgh, having to stop at the bottom of Lothian Road,
close to the western end of Princes Street, which it took as the name for
its terminus. Nevertheless, by 1850 the NBR provided a link to the
north of England and eventually this became the East Coast Main Line.
The opening of a branch to Hawick later led the way, through the
Border Union Railway, to Carlisle, giving the NBR a second route over
the border and Edinburgh a second route to Carlisle, and south, via the
Midland Railway. The last major link in the network of railways in and
around Edinburgh followed in 1890 with the completion of the Forth
Bridge, which meant that the city sat astride the most direct route
between Aberdeen and London. Meanwhile, the Caledonian linked

with the London & North Western Railway at Carlisle to provide what became the West Coast Main Line.

Included in the Edinburgh network were a number of suburban and country branches, with lines opened to Polton and North Berwick in 1850, Peebles in 1855, Dolphinton in 1864, Penicuik in 1876 and Gullane in 1898. There was also a link line to Galashiels, while a light railway was opened to Gifford in 1901. Eventually, a number of routes of varying degrees of directness linked Edinburgh and Glasgow. In 1884, the NBR opened the Edinburgh & District Suburban Railway. The inner suburban railways soon suffered from competition from electric trams, and this was especially true of the EDSR, which was laid out as an oval and so often did not provide the most direct route between two points.

Most of these lines terminated at Waverley, which became very congested and needed rebuilding in 1890. It was rebuilt again in 2007. A new station at Leith was opened to ease the pressure on Waverley, but Leith Central was not convenient for most of the passenger traffic, and especially not for the first-class traveller looking for an express. Both the NBR and the Caledonian built branches into the docks at Leith.

The NBR had two locomotive sheds in Edinburgh, at Haymarket and St Margaret's, but after merging with the Edinburgh & Glasgow, it transferred most of its heavy work to Cowlairs at Glasgow.

Glasgow
Often known as the 'Workshop of the British Empire', Glasgow, the largest city in Scotland with twice Edinburgh's population, was one of the world's leading industrial cities during the nineteenth century, with a substantial proportion of the world's merchant shipping built on the Clyde. This was not a one-industry city, however, and its engineering activities included several major railway locomotive works, some of which were independent. Later commercial vehicles were also built, while lighter engineering included the Singer sewing machine factory and cotton mills and breweries. These industries and the surrounding coal mines were served by a rudimentary network of tramroads developed during the eighteenth century.

Glasgow's first railway was the Garnkirk & Glasgow, opened in 1831, which soon built an extension to a temporary wooden terminus at Buchanan Street, which was taken over by the Caledonian Railway, initially for its services to Aberdeen, although it later also became the terminus for services to London Euston. The city soon became a focal point for a growing number of railways, with the next being the Glasgow Paisley Kilmarnock & Ayr, which shared a terminus at Bridge Street, south of the Clyde, with the Glasgow Paisley & Greenock. North of the river was the Edinburgh & Glasgow's Queen Street Station, initially reached by a cable-working from Cowlairs.

Initially, the Clyde proved to be a major barrier, with the north and the south of the city kept separate, partly because of Admiralty objections to a fixed bridge. The river was not bridged until 1876, when the Glasgow & South Western sent its line into St Enoch, also the terminus for Midland Railway services from London St Pancras. In 1879, the CR opened Glasgow Central Station. The North British Railway was able to use land vacated by the University as it sought more suitable premises, and also had the support of the city council in demolishing some particularly bad slums, in building its sidings and sheds, while it used Queen Street, acquired with the EGR. Between 1885 and 1910, the rival companies each built their own competing lines into the docks and many industrial areas. Suburban and even urban routes proliferated, and included the Glasgow Subway, a circular route initially worked by cable.

Glasgow was the only city outside London to have a Royal Commission on its railways, but unlike that in London, which imposed an inner limit on construction of new surface lines and termini, that in Glasgow had no effect. The city's industry contributed much, and the CR in particular was predominantly a freight railway, but even so passenger numbers at Central Station rose from 4.75 million in 1880 to reach 15.75 million in 1897. The termini included hotels, such as the St Enoch Hotel at the Glasgow & South Western terminus, which when opened was the largest hotel in Scotland. Suburban lines developed on a scale second only to London, including the famous 'Cathcart Circle', albeit never a true circle, which operated out of Glasgow Central. The expansion of Central between 1901 and 1905 took it over Argyll Street, which famously became a meeting place for exiled Highlanders, known as the Highlandman's Umbrella, or, in the local patois, *'Hielanman's Umbrella'*.

As with other major cities, passenger numbers began to fall as the urban and inner suburban networks proved vulnerable to competition, first from the electric tram, and then, after the First World War from the motor bus. Cathcart Circle or not, traffic at Central began to decline from 1905 onwards. Glasgow also began to lose its competitive edge, with heavy industry beginning a slow decline, while the 1926 Miners' Strike hit demand for coal particularly hard. To counter this, new stations were opened close to new residential or industrial developments. The Glasgow Subway was taken over by the City and electrified between the wars.

Grouping had little impact on the pattern of railway services. There was some rationalization of the networks to the south-west, mainly favouring the former GSWR lines rather than those of the rival CR, but plans to rationalize the four termini – Buchanan Street, which would have been enlarged, Central, Queen Street and St Enoch – into two failed, for regardless of the economies that could have been made and the improved convenience for passengers, the money was simply not available. Another plan never implemented was to expand the Glasgow Subway.

Chapter 3

The Competitors

Prior to 1923, Britain's railways were fragmented, although in practice this was only a serious problem in a few cases. The railway companies competed, but they also collaborated. As we will see later, the Midland Railway competed with both the East and West Coast companies for traffic between London and Scotland, but it joined its East Coast rivals to help finance the great bridge across the Firth of Forth.

A great facilitator of collaboration and coordination was the Railway Clearing House, which dated from 1842. In essence, it was there so that the railway companies could pay or collect monies due from trains running over each other's lines, or for passengers who had booked a through ticket using the services of two or more companies. Trains would also often have carriages or wagons from more than one company. This made through running much easier. The RCH, as it became known, worked hard to standardize signals and headcodes, again helping through running, but even the RCH could never come down firmly on a single standard braking system, so vacuum and air-brakes persisted throughout the network.

The East Coast Main Line, as it is known today, was the territory of the Great Northern Railway (GNR), at its southern end with its terminus at King's Cross, becoming that of the North Eastern Railway (NER) at York, and while the track transferred from the NER to the third member of the group, the North British Railway, at Berwick, the proud NER insisted that its locomotives continued unchanged all the way from York to Edinburgh Waverley.

Across the country, the West Coast Main Line, again a modern term, was the property of the London & North Western from Euston all the way to Carlisle, within a few miles of the border between England and Scotland. At Carlisle, it became the Caledonian Railway's main line to Glasgow Queen Street.

Just as the Caledonian had its own station in Edinburgh at Princes Street, behind the Caledonian Hotel at the western end of the street, the North British ran into Glasgow at Queen Street.

The newcomer or interloper was the Midland Railway, running all the way from St Pancras to the Scottish borders, where its partner was the Glasgow & South-Western, whose locomotives pulled the Midland Railway's proud red rolling stock all the way to St Enoch, while the North British did the same for trains to Edinburgh and, later, Aberdeen.

The companies had different strengths and weaknesses, with the East Coast companies having the shortest route between London and Edinburgh and, when the Forth and the Tay were bridged, between London and Aberdeen. Fewer steep gradients existed on the East Coast run, although there were some between Newcastle and Edinburgh, and the line through Fife between the Forth and the Tay was difficult, with many curves and gradients, and inconveniently-placed speed restrictions. The West Coast, despite the steep summits of Shap and Beattock, was among the first to introduce water troughs so that locomotives could pick up water on the move – an aid to longer distances between stops first introduced in 1860 on the London & North Western Railway. Without water troughs, locomotives had to stop every 80–100 miles to 'imbibe' water. Water troughs were not suitable for slow-moving trains, as there had to be enough pressure to force water upwards into the tank, and not suitable for tank engines, as the pressure of the water tended to split the tanks.

Changing Locomotives
The locomotives of the day were in a period of transition. In 1888, most of the locomotives were still 'single-wheelers' with a large driving wheel as big as 8ft in diameter in some cases, but by 1895 compound engines with two driving wheels, usually in a 4–4–0 configuration, were becoming commonplace. 'Compound' referred to the fact that steam entered one cylinder and worked a piston, which then enabled the steam to pass into an adjoining cylinder, working another piston. Such locomotives became practical when steel technology advanced to the stage that connecting rods could be used to couple the driving wheels.

Generally, the more driving wheels the better, and as power increased, four, six, or even eight or ten driving wheels were needed. Nevertheless, at the time, the 'balance of power' was not always with the locomotive with more driving wheels, and not all of the locomotives used in the races were new – there was much to be said for using a proven locomotive. Until power requirements made multiple driving wheels essential, single-wheelers could often show a fine performance, partly because the larger wheel had a greater rolling contact area with the track, and partly because research since has shown that with a 4–4–0, the first set of driving wheels depressed the rails very slightly, so that the second set did not have the same grip and tractive effort. The races were, of course, well before the days of the six coupled driving wheels and these took some time to become established as efficient means of traction.

The East Coast Companies
As an indication of how things were, the East Coast group of companies, as already mentioned, included the North British, North Eastern and Great Northern railway companies. Nevertheless, through trains and even through carriages ran over the network, so that not only were direct links between Scotland's three largest cities and London maintained, but through carriages ran all the way from Aberdeen to Penzance, the latter on the Great Western Railway. Locomotives changed along the way, mainly because of the need for coal, as water could be picked up at stations or even, at speed, from water troughs while the train was on the move, although the East Coast companies lagged behind the West Coast in the provision of water troughs, as we will see later.

The Anglo-Scottish services were not the only traffic, and the line had to accommodate traffic to and from the ports of Humberside, the Yorkshire coalfields and the agriculture and fisheries traffic that originated in East Anglia. Passenger traffic was important, especially into East Anglian resorts, but the companies involved were among the most dependent of any main line on goods traffic.

Great Northern Railway
Originating as the London & York Railway, authorized in 1846 in the face of heavy opposition, the GNR title was adopted by the following year despite the fact that York was its most northerly destination. The first services used a leased section of line between Louth and Grimsby from 1848, but the main line opened between a temporary station at Maiden Lane, London, and Peterborough, and between Doncaster and York, in 1850, by which time it was also able to serve all of the important centres in the West Riding. It was in 1852 that the through line between London and Doncaster was completed along with King's Cross, while the main works at Doncaster came in 1853. Other smaller

companies were acquired or running powers taken so that the GNR served Bradford, Cambridge, Halifax, Leeds and Nottingham, and, with an agreement with the Manchester Sheffield & Lincolnshire Railway, which later became the Great Central, express services from London to Manchester started in 1857. The following year the Midland Railway ran over the GNR line south of Hitchin to London, helping to undermine the 'Euston Square Confederacy' sponsored by the London & North Western Railway.

The revenue from the Yorkshire coal traffic attracted the jealous attention of the Great Eastern and the Lancashire & Yorkshire, who twice attempted unsuccessfully to promote a bill through Parliament for a trunk line from Doncaster through Lincolnshire. In the meantime, the GNR improved its position by joining the MSLR in buying the West Riding & Grimsby Railway, linking Doncaster with Wakefield. In 1865, with the MSLR, both companies promoted a Manchester–Liverpool line, and expanded into Lancashire and Cheshire through the Cheshire Lines Committee with the Midland. In 1879, it joined the GER in the Great Northern & Great Eastern Joint lines between Huntingdon and Doncaster, a route that required some new construction.

GNR main line services were reliable and punctual, especially after Henry Oakley became general manager in 1870. It was soon running more expresses than either the LNWR or MR, including some of the world's fastest, hauled by Patrick Stirling's famous single driving-wheel locomotives, appropriately known as 'Stirling Singles'. The intensity of service required block signalling and interlocking, while stations and goods sidings had to be enlarged and working improved. By 1873, it had reached a peak of profitability, but for the rest of the decade, investment grew more quickly than revenue and, especially in the extension of the Cheshire Lines network, the company risked over-extending itself. In the East Midlands it constructed new lines jointly with the LNWR, to some extent spurred by an earlier rates war with the Midland, although in 1889, together with the MR, it acquired the Eastern & Midlands Railway, creating the Midland & Great Northern Joint Railway.

Earlier, the creation of through services on the East Coast Main Line was helped in 1860 when the East Coast Joint Stock, a common pool of passenger vehicles, was created by the GNR, North Eastern and North British. In 1862, the first through express services from King's Cross to Edinburgh Waverley started, with the 10.00am departure in each direction being named the 'Flying Scotsman' from the 1870s, by which time the company was also able to reach Glasgow over the North British Railway. The first regular restaurant cars appeared in 1879 and continuous vacuum braking from 1881. The company later introduced the first fully-fitted goods trains. As traffic and the weight of trains increased, the entire route had to be relaid with heavier rails from the mid-1890s, with widening at the southern end of the route, while heavier trains were worked by H.A. Ivatt's new locomotives. From 1905 Nigel Gresley designed new carriages, including some using articulation to improve the ride and reduce weight.

The company also expanded its London suburban traffic, not only from King's Cross but also using Broad Street as a convenient City terminus in conjunction with the North London Railway.

North British Railway

The North British was authorized in 1844 after the York & North Midland Railway was persuaded by George Hudson to provide £50,000 to complete an East Coast line between Edinburgh and London. Hudson's intervention was necessary after Scottish investors had failed to provide sufficient capital. The line opened over the fifty-seven miles to Berwick-on-Tweed in 1846, but had been poorly constructed and, within three months, floods swept away many weak bridges and undermined embankments. Despite this, the NBR built branches to Duns, North Berwick and Hawick, with the last providing a link via Carlisle, the 'Waverley' route, with the West Coast line when it opened in 1862. In return for allowing the North Eastern Railway to run over its line between Berwick and Edinburgh, the NBR was allowed running powers between Newcastle and Hexham.

After an extremely shaky start, with poor punctuality and scant dividends, Richard Hodgson became chairman in 1855 and began to rebuild the company's operations. It acquired the Edinburgh Perth & Dundee Railway in 1862, and the Edinburgh & Glasgow Railway in 1864 in the face of fierce competition from its stronger rival, the Caledonian. Hodgson's reign ended in 1866 when it was discovered that he was falsifying the accounts in order to pay an improved dividend, and his departure nearly led to a merger with the Caledonian but for a shareholders' revolt. It was not until the completion of the Settle & Carlisle line by the Midland Railway in 1876, allowing through trains from St Pancras to reach Edinburgh over the Waverley route, that the company's circumstances improved. Dugald Drummond, the NBR's locomotive superintendent, designed a new 4–4–0 express locomotive to handle the Anglo-Scottish expresses, before he was poached by the Caledonian in 1882.

Competition with the Caledonian continued and proved ruinous. Both companies wanted the lucrative Fife coal market and both wanted to be the best route to Aberdeen, while the NBR wanted its share of the growing Glasgow commuter traffic. Both companies built large and prestigious hotels, with the NBR's flagship being that at Waverley Station, originally known as the 'North British' but now known by the more acceptable name of the New Balmoral. Still more ambitious was the effort made to create a port and resort at Silloth in Cumberland, which also included building much of the town as well as a hotel and golf course. The port attracted ferry services to Ireland and the Isle of Man, but the resort failed. Rather more success was enjoyed in developing the resort of North Berwick. The company later bought the port of Methil in Fife to handle shipments of coal from the local coalfields. The NBR even attempted to compete with the CR on the Clyde, initially putting two ferries into service in 1866, but soon had to withdraw them, and a second attempt, based on Dunoon, saw heavy losses. A later attempt in conjunction with the Glasgow & South Western saw steamer services from Greenock, while steamers were also operated on Loch Lomond after the NBR purchased a local company.

The heavily indented coastline of Eastern Scotland meant that the North British had substantial ferry operations of its own across both the Forth and the Tay until bridges could be built across these two wide estuaries. The first attempt at building the Tay Bridge resulted in disaster, with the bridge collapsing in a storm while a train was crossing on 28 December 1879, with the loss of all seventy-two people aboard.

A new bridge was built and this was followed by the imposing Forth Bridge, completed in 1890. The heavy cost of building a new Tay Bridge left the NBR short of money and so the Forth Bridge was a partnership between the company and both the NER and GNR, as well as the ambitious Midland Railway, which was keen to extend its competition with the East and West Coast routes all the way to Aberdeen. Once completed, these two bridges meant that the NBR line was the fastest and most direct route to Dundee and Aberdeen. However, unfortunately the line through Fife linking the two bridges was not rebuilt, which became an obstacle to fast through running, especially in the 'Race to Aberdeen' of 1895. At no time could the company manage to persuade the NER to allow it to handle expresses from London on the stretch of line between Berwick-on-Tweed and Edinburgh.

Traffic boomed, however, with heavy congestion at Waverley that required the station to be rebuilt and the tracks to Haymarket, with the intervening tunnels, quadrupled, with the result that when the rebuilt station opened with its suburban platforms in 1898, it was claimed to be second only to Waterloo in size. Freight traffic also grew, and shipments of coal through the port of Methil rose from 400,000 tons in 1888 to 2.8 million tons twenty years later.

While most of the railway network had been completed by 1880, the NBR had two of the last major railway projects in the country prior to the Channel Tunnel Rail Link. The first of these was the West Highland Line, which ran from Craigendoran, west of Glasgow, to Fort William, and opened in 1894, and then the extension to Mallaig, completed in 1901, but which had taken Robert McAlpine four years for just forty miles and, almost uniquely in Great Britain, had needed a subsidy of £260,000 (about £17.5 million today) of taxpayers' money. These were followed by a line from Dunfermline to Kincardine and a small number of light railways, essentially infilling gaps in the system.

Despite its seeming poverty, the NBR was the largest Scottish railway company, contributing 1,300 track miles, 1,100 locomotives, 3,500 carriages and 57,000 wagons to the new London & North Eastern Railway on 1 January 1923.

North Eastern Railway
The largest and most profitable of the companies brought together to form the LNER, with 1,757 route miles, the North Eastern Railway was formed in 1854 when four railway companies merged their operations: the York Newcastle & Berwick, the York & North Midland, the Leeds Northern and the tiny Malton & Driffield Junction. The three larger companies did not merge their shareholdings until 1870. The NER came into being with 700 route miles, but was not a complete rationalization of railway operations in the North-East, as four other companies in the area remained independent for the best part of ten years.

One of the independent companies was the Stockton & Darlington, which had supported the construction of the South Durham &

Lancashire Union line, allied with the London & North Western Railway, but after the SDR and SDLUR merged, they were taken over by the NER in 1863. Similar action was taken by the West Hartlepool Railway, which served a port that was a strong competitor to Hull and Middlesbrough, and sought an alliance with the LNWR, planning to compete with the NER, and it was not until 1865 that it agreed to be taken over. That year the Newcastle & Carlisle was also absorbed. This left just the Blyth & Tyne as an independent company within the NER area, and this was not absorbed until 1874. The acquisition of these companies was often difficult and, once in NER ownership, integration proved to be slow and difficult.

The NER was a vital link in the line from London to Edinburgh, linking the Great Northern in the south with the North British Railway at Berwick-on-Tweed, which formed what is now the East Coast Main Line. Between 1868 and 1871, it built cut-offs amounting to twenty-six miles, with the two main ones being one between Durham and Gateshead and between Doncaster and York. Nevertheless, the NER was slow to introduce the block system of signalling and interlocking of points and signals and these, as well as management failings, contributed to the four accidents suffered in late 1870. William O'Brien, the general manager, was sacked and Henry Tennant succeeded him, making the necessary reforms both to the structure of the company and to its operating practices. Despite these difficulties the newly-integrated company managed to pay a dividend of more than eight per cent during the 1870s. It also mounted 'The Jubilee of the Railway System' at Darlington on the SDR's fiftieth anniversary in 1875. The stubborn and independent streak shown by the railway meant that it was the last of the trunk railways to abandon iron rails in favour of steel, although it could be argued that this was to appease the powerful iron masters. Nevertheless, it also refused to send a delegate to the Railway Clearing House to discuss standardizing railway telegraph codes, as it would not consider any revision of its own codes.

The NER's monopoly in the north-east soon came under threat. Hull Corporation was angered by the NER entering into a traffic-pooling agreement for freight receipts for all of the ports between the Tyne and the Humber. The Corporation backed plans for a new dock to ease congestion on the Humber, and a new independent railway to bring coal from south and west Yorkshire. Originating as the Hull, Barnsley

& West Riding Junction Railway & Dock Company, but later becoming the Hull & Barnsley Railway, the new sixty-six-mile line was authorized in 1880. Railway and new docks were both completed in 1885. A rates war ensued, which forced the Hull & Barnsley into receivership during 1887–89, but an agreement was reached and, while the NER was never able to acquire the HBR, the two companies shared construction of the large new deep-water dock, the King George V, which opened in 1914.

The 1870s were not a period of easy growth for the railways, and the financial performance of the NER is all the more creditable for this. Faced with a recession in mineral traffic, the company began to encourage third-class travel.

The NER gained momentum and prominence when Tennant was superseded by G.S. Gibb in 1891. Gibb believed in building a management team with diverse experience rather than continuing the NER's own introspective policies, and recruited R.L. Wedgwood, Frank Pick and E.C. Geddes, all of whom later rose to prominence in the industry. Gibb changed the NER's working statistics, using ton-mileage rather than train-mileage to assess performance. At first other companies were dubious about the changes, introduced in 1899, but in due course these became the industry standard. Forward thinking was also evident when the NER became the first railway to negotiate with trade unions on hours and wages. Gibb himself moved on in 1906, becoming managing director of London's Underground group of companies.

Wedgwood became the first Chief General Manager of the LNER. Geddes moved into politics, became first Minister of Transport and was largely responsible for forcing through grouping of the railways, before moving into the manufacturing industry.

Meanwhile, a succession of chief mechanical engineers, starting with Wilson Wordsdell, followed by Thomas Wordsdell and Vincent Raven, took the company into electrification. It started with the Quayside freight line at Newcastle in 1902, and then the suburban system north of the city in 1904, and by 1915 had also electrified the longer-distance line from Shildon to Middlesbrough. The company even planned for electrification of the ECML between York and Newcastle, but in the end this was shelved due to grouping and nationalization and did not take place until 1991. Nevertheless, the NER passed on to the LNER fifty-eight route miles of electrified line, albeit in three separate schemes, and a total of 126 multiple-unit motor coaches and trailers, and thirteen electric engines in three separate classes. Had Raven's ideas been supported by the LNER, electrification could have come earlier, but it would have required a chief general manager with a determination to electrify, along the lines of the Southern Railway's Walker, for this to have happened.

The HBR was finally absorbed by the NER in 1922.

The West Coast Companies

As with the East Coast route, the Anglo-Scottish expresses were not the only traffic, for this line carried important traffic between England and Ireland, with the line from Chester to Holyhead for the packet services to Dublin, and from Dumfries to Stranraer for the services to Larne and on by train to Belfast. The important cities of the north-west, such as Liverpool and Manchester, also provided significant traffic flows, as did Birmingham and the coalfields of the Midlands. The railways were not only concerned about their own shipping services, but also advertised and linked their services with those of other operators, such as B&I from Liverpool to Dublin and the Belfast Steamship Company's service from Belfast, both of which later became part of the Coast Lines Group.

Caledonian Railway

The largest Scottish company to be merged into the LMS, the Caledonian Railway adopted the Royal Arms of Scotland as its crest and its locomotives were smartly presented in a blue livery. It was founded in 1845 to extend the West Coast Main Line from Carlisle to Glasgow and Edinburgh, dividing at Carstairs, and at the time it was expected to be the only Anglo-Scottish line. The engineer was Joseph Locke. Initially, grand termini were planned in both cities, as well as a cross-country line, but these plans were thwarted.

The company reached Glasgow over the metals of the Garnkirk & Glasgow (later renamed the Glasgow & Coatbridge) and the Wishaw & Coltness railways to Buchanan Street station, whose wooden train sheds remained until after grouping. Eventually three Glasgow termini were used, including, from 1849, the South Side station accessed via the Clydesdale Junction and the Glasgow Barrhead & Neilston Direct, while the CR also shared Bridge Street with the Glasgow & South Western. South Side was closed when Central and St Enoch were opened in the 1870s, but Bridge Street continued to be used until 1906, after Central had been extended, eventually having seventeen platforms on two levels.

The line was extended north to Aberdeen using the Scottish Central, Scottish Midland Junction and Aberdeen Railways, and in 1856 the last two merged to form the Scottish North Eastern Railway, before all three were absorbed by the Caledonian in 1865–66. From 1880, the Caledonian served the Western Highlands over the Callander & Oban Railway, which it effectively rescued and developed, and then, up to 1900, built a network of lines along the Clyde to compete with the Glasgow & South Western and North British railways, giving the company a suburban and tourist network as well as serving steamer services, and the growing shipyards on the Clyde and the mines of Lanarkshire, for which many new lines and private sidings were built. The Caledonian's main routes were the finest in Scotland. The company moved into steamer services, including tourist steamers on Loch Lomond, with the main steamer-railway terminus on the Clyde being at Wemyss Bay. The further expansion of the Glasgow suburban network was cut short by the appearance of horse and, later, electric trams, with the Paisley & District line completed, but never opened for passenger trains.

Meanwhile, in Edinburgh the unsatisfactory Lothian Road station was replaced by Princes Street, which later had the Caledonian Hotel added, providing an impressive frontage, which is all that remains for the casual observer to see. A network of suburban services was also created in the capital. Further north, the company built its own station at Stirling and took the lead in remodelling the joint stations at Perth and Aberdeen, and opened new tourist lines from Crieff to Lochearnhead and from Connel to Ballachulish.

The company provided railway links for all of the docks within its wide operating area, as well as owning those at Grangemouth, which it acquired with the Forth & Clyde Canal in 1867.

Intense competition arose with the Glasgow & South Western and, especially after the opening of the East Coast Main Line, the North British, initially for traffic between Edinburgh and London, although after the Tay and Forth bridges were completed the rivalry extended to Aberdeen. The hotel business extended from Glasgow and Edinburgh to include the famous hotel at Gleneagles. The company became famous for good design and high standards, with a strong awareness of the importance of public image. When merged into the London Midland & Scottish Railway in 1923, it contributed 1,057 route miles.

London & North Western Railway

Formed in 1846 by an amalgamation of the London & Birmingham, Grand Junction and Manchester & Birmingham Railways, initially the LNWR consisted of 247 trunk route miles stretching as far north as Preston, with through running over other lines to Carlisle, while also serving Liverpool and Manchester. Lacking a regional base and vulnerable to competition, the LNWR immediately set about establishing alliances and acquiring other lines along its route. The first major alliance was known as the Euston Square Confederacy, formed in 1850, and was a defensive measure against the Great Northern. This was followed by the Octuple Agreement, pooling receipts for traffic between London and points north of York, which in turn was replaced by the English & Scotch Traffic Agreement, which ran from 1859 to 1869 and gave Glasgow traffic to the LNWR's West Coast route and that to Edinburgh to the East Coast.

In the meantime, by 1859 the LNWR had added Cambridge, Leeds, Oxford and Peterborough to its network, while also leasing the Lancaster & Carlisle Railway, and concluded an alliance with the Caledonian Railway, so that the West Coast Main Line served not only Glasgow, but also Edinburgh and Aberdeen. It had also acquired the Chester & Holyhead Railway and the major share of the traffic to Ireland through both Holyhead and Liverpool, where in 1864 the company acquired the dock at Garston, which was enlarged in 1896, mainly for coal to Ireland. Later, it reached the Cumberland coast and started running through mid-Wales, establishing a cross-country service from Shrewsbury to Swansea and Carmarthen, largely run over its own lines. This was followed by a further cross-country service from Hereford to Cardiff and Newport, and the acquisition of a number of branch lines in South Wales. In the London area, it acquired the North London Railway, which retained its identity as a subsidiary, and used a number of lines in west London operated jointly with the Great Western that enabled it to bypass the capital and operate through to the south. In 1847, the Trent Valley line opened, bypassing Birmingham, and this was followed by another line in 1864 that bypassed major junctions at Winwick and Golborne. In 1869 a direct line was opened to Liverpool through Runcorn.

From 1861, all locomotive building was concentrated on Crewe, while the works at Wolverton that had built locomotives for the Southern Division before it was merged with the Northern Division concentrated on carriage building. Crewe also included a steelworks and produced the company's rails, at the time longer than any other railway in the British Isles at 60ft, helping to provide the smoother ride and high-quality permanent way in which the company took such pride. Eventually, almost everything from soap and tickets to signalling equipment was produced 'in-house'.

Crewe became the ultimate company town, with the LNWR providing the services that would normally be provided by a local authority. The chief mechanical engineer from 1871 to 1903, F.W. Webb, took the existing stock of 2–2–2 and 2–4–0 locomotives, added many more of the latter, and then started to build compound locomotives and the first 0–8–0 freight locomotives in Britain.

Despite collaboration with the GWR in London, competition developed on traffic to Birmingham and Merseyside. In an attempt to secure its position, the LNWR proposed a merger with the Midland Railway, but this failed and further competition resulted when the Midland managed to reach London over the GNR. A planned merger with the North Staffordshire Railway also failed. By 1869, there was heavy competition with the MR, and later the Great Central, for Manchester business. This extended to Anglo-Scottish traffic once the Midland completed its Settle and Carlisle line in 1875.

A far happier relationship flourished with the Lancashire & Yorkshire Railway, despite competition between Liverpool and Manchester, and in 1863 the two companies established a series of traffic pooling agreements. Parliament rejected a merger in 1872, but in 1908 the two companies and the MR agreed to send freight consignments by the shortest route. Freight was important to the LNWR, and at Liverpool it operated no fewer than six goods depots. In 1882, it pioneered gravity-operated marshalling yards at Edge Hill. The mixture of slow freight traffic and fast expresses led the company to quadruple its tracks and, when this was not possible, to provide a double-track alternative. By 1914, eighty-nine per cent of the 209 miles between Euston and Preston was covered in this way, as well as much of the route to Holyhead and to Leeds. Flying junctions, of which the first was at Weaver Junction, north of Crewe, also accelerated traffic and reduced conflicting movements.

While the company invested in shipping as well as railways and ports, it did not acquire the mail contract from Holyhead to Ireland until 1920. Previously, political considerations had left this with the City of Dublin Steam Packet Company. The LNWR had worked hard for forty years to gain this business, building a new harbour and quays at North Wall, Dublin, as well as building faster ships. The reward in the interval was a major share of cattle and freight traffic across the Irish Sea. Earlier, in an attempt to gain the traffic between Great Britain and Belfast, the company took a majority shareholding in the Dundalk Newry & Greenore Railway, and in 1873 had started a shipping service to Greenore. Perhaps more successful was the joint operation with the LYR from Fleetwood to Belfast and from Stranraer in Scotland to Larne with the Midland, Caledonian and Glasgow & South Western.

Despite the length of its trunk route to Scotland, the chairman between 1861 and 1891, Sir Richard Moon, believed that excessive speed used too much coal and argued that 40mph was sufficient. Nevertheless, a step forward in comfort came with bogie carriages in the late 1880s, and these were followed by all-corridor trains for the Scottish services in 1893. Another move to improve the comfort of passengers was the adoption of 'club' carriages, pioneered by the Lancashire & Yorkshire on some of its commuter trains from Blackpool to Manchester, with the LNWR adding a service from North Wales. Passengers had to be elected to membership of the club carriages, and while initially they were only first class, second-class club carriages made an appearance later. Liverpool was the major port for transatlantic traffic at the time, and special twelve-wheel carriages were built for the boat trains, but eventually most of the transatlantic shipping services, with the exception of those of Canadian Pacific, transferred to Southampton. Between 1914 and 1922, the LNWR electrified its suburban services from Euston and Broad Street to Watford, using the third and fourth rail system favoured by the Underground group of companies, and after grouping these were extended to Rickmansworth.

In the year before the grouping, the LNWR finally merged with the LYR, using the LNWR name, a move intended to strengthen its influence in the eventual grouping in 1923. At that point the LNWR was one of the three largest railways in the British Isles and contributed 2,066 route miles to the LMS.

The Midland Route

Very much the latecomer, the Midland Railway had massive ambitions, although not so ambitious as to abandon its home in Derby for a base in London. It was the only railway company serving the capital that did not have its headquarters there. In some ways it is peripheral to this story of competition between the two fastest lines, but it is relevant as its longer route did provide competition of a different sort, offering comfort rather than speed. After the races ended in 1895, it was the Midland which almost provoked a new set of races early in the new century. It was also the better railway for those intending to travel to Ireland, either via its own port at Heysham, from which ferries crossed to Belfast, or along the 'Port Road', the railway line linking Dumfries with the port of Stranraer, with a ferry route to Larne in Northern Ireland, where the Midland had taken over the Belfast & Northern Counties Railway. As with the other lines, the Midland route required more than one company to be involved, and it teamed up with the Glasgow & South Western Railway and the North British Railway, the main competitors in Scotland to the Caledonian Railway.

Glasgow & South Western Railway

This was formed in 1850 when the Glasgow Paisley Kilmarnock & Ayr Railway, authorized in 1837, acquired the Glasgow Dumfries & Carlisle Railway. The line to Ayr had been completed in 1840, and was followed in 1843 by a branch from Dalry to Kilmarnock, but this eventually became the main line to Carlisle via Dumfries. It had less severe gradients than the rival Caledonian line to Carlisle via Beattock, but was eighteen miles longer. For the remainder of the nineteenth century, the company acquired other lines in its area, including Scotland's first railway, the Kilmarnock & Troon, dating from 1811. It built the first railway hotel for golfers at Turnberry in 1906. The main works were at Kilmarnock, completed in 1856, but a new workshop at Barassie, near Troon, was completed in 1901.

The main business of the railway was the movement of coal and tourist and commuter traffic to the resorts on the Ayrshire coast, while it also handled a substantial volume of traffic to Ireland. It was forced to operate the 'Port Road', the lines from Dumfries to Portpatrick, and later Stranraer, when that became the main Scottish port for Ireland, in partnership with the Caledonian, London & North Western and Midland Railways. Financial and operational difficulties delayed completion of the Glasgow–Stranraer route until 1877 and it was not fully incorporated into the GSWR until 1892. The problems were caused partly by competition for Irish traffic by ports in Ayrshire, and by the fact that at the time it was also possible to sail directly from Glasgow to Belfast and other Irish ports, including Dublin and Londonderry.

In Glasgow, through running to the North British became possible when the City Union railway was completed in 1870, and through running to the Midland Railway's Settle and Carlisle started once this route was completed. Parliament rejected plans for a merger with the Midland, but the two companies collaborated on express services from St Pancras to St Enoch, completed in 1876. Strong competition developed with the Caledonian in Ayrshire, and joint operation of a new direct Glasgow–Kilmarnock line was forced on the companies when it opened in 1873. A bid for the GSWR by the CR was rejected by Parliament in 1890. Quadrupling of the thirty miles from Glasgow to Kilwinning was largely completed by the outbreak of the First World War.

Midland Railway

Authorized in 1844, the Midland Railway resulted from the amalgamation of the Birmingham & Derby Junction, Midland Counties and North Midland railways, and had George Hudson, the 'Railway King', as its first chairman. This was the first significant merger of railway companies sanctioned by Parliament. Initially, the Midland was a regional railway without its own access to London, and acted as a link between the London & Birmingham at Rugby and the York & North Midland, another Hudson railway, at Normanton. Initially, the MR had a monopoly of traffic from London to the North East, but a more direct line, the Great Northern, was authorized in 1846 and opened throughout in 1852.

Nevertheless, the MR had by this time started its own programme of expansion, reaching Lincoln in 1846, and that year leasing the Leeds & Bradford Railway, which was authorized to extend to Skipton, where it would connect with the North Western Railway (not to be confused with the LNWR) line to Lancaster and Morecambe. The MR itself reached Peterborough in 1848, and then acquired the Birmingham & Gloucester and the Bristol & Gloucester. Nevertheless, expansion was soon checked by the stock market crisis of 1847–48, and then by Hudson's downfall in 1849 after he was discovered to be paying dividends out of capital to attract investors.

Hudson's successor was John Ellis, who provided the steady hand the company needed. The MR then started a period of profitable operation, and even paid a dividend in the difficult period of 1849–51, with an average of four per cent paid up to 1859, and then more than six per cent during the 1860s.

The relationship with the NWR had not worked as well as the MR had anticipated and the decision was taken to build its own line between Settle and Carlisle, which was authorized in 1866. This was poor timing as it followed a collapse in the stock market. The MR tried to abandon the project, but the North British and the Lancashire & Yorkshire Railways, which had supported the measure, managed to persuade the MR to press ahead, although the line took ten years to complete because of extensive engineering works, including the Ribblehead Viaduct. Meanwhile, the MR reached Manchester in 1867, running through the Peak District and with running powers over the Manchester Sheffield and Lincolnshire Railway, forerunner of the Great Central. Next, the MR headed towards London, initially with a line from Leicester to Bedford and Hitchin, where it connected with the GNR and acquired rights to run to King's Cross. Finding this far from satisfactory, it then built a line from Bedford to London, where it opened its terminus at St Pancras in 1868. It was intended at one time that the head office should move from Derby to London once St Pancras was completed, but this did not happen and instead the building at the London terminus became a hotel. Derby did enjoy another innovation when, in 1910, a central control office was created in an attempt to improve the poor punctuality of the MR's trains.

The Settle & Carlisle Line and the St Pancras extension were part of a £6 million investment programme, equating to at least £350 million today, although given the high cost of property in the London area, the real figure today would probably be very much higher. This organic growth was not the sole way forward, as the MR sought to expand. In 1875, it joined the London & South Western Railway in leasing the Somerset & Dorset, enabling it to reach Bournemouth on the South Coast. The following year, running powers were acquired that enabled the MR to reach the coalfields of South Wales.

In 1872, the MR announced that it would carry third-class passengers on all of its trains, a revolutionary move at a time when many railways regarded third-class as a nuisance. In 1875, it announced that it was scrapping second class, which meant that third-class passengers enjoyed the comfort of former second-class rolling stock, and at the same time cut first-class fares. While this was intended to put competitors at a disadvantage, many other companies retained second class, which survived on the former Great Eastern London suburban services and on some Continental boat trains between the two world wars. The MR's move had another advantage, for while it could reach

Edinburgh and Glasgow by way of the Settle & Carlisle, it was a longer route, and by providing a more comfortable service it could compete once through running started in 1876. A further step in ensuring the comfort of passengers followed a visit to the USA by the competitive general manager, James Allport, in 1874, which had him persuade the board to introduce Pullman cars, for which a supplementary fare could be charged: once restaurant and Pullman cars did start running on the MR, the company gained a good reputation for its food.

While the MR certainly took passenger traffic very seriously, it was also a major freight railway, and this part of its operations actually increased with the extension to London. It was amongst the first to attempt to purchase the private owners' wagons that used its rails, and while not completely successful, this was certainly a measure approved of by most railway managers.

Despite the excellence of its facilities at Derby, the MR had no hesitation in buying locomotive or rolling stock from other sources when quality, innovation or price made this attractive. Nevertheless, the company had just two locomotive superintendents between 1844 and 1903, Matthew Kirtley and S.W. Johnson. It inherited its engineer, W.H. Barlow, from the MCR in 1844, but he remained until 1857, and then continued as a consultant, building St Pancras. He was succeeded by J.S. Crossley, who was responsible for the Settle & Carlisle line. The magnificent engineering of the Settle & Carlisle and the grand St Pancras, however, were in contrast to the MR's policies on locomotives, which were relatively straightforward and smaller than those appearing on other railways during the late nineteenth and early twentieth centuries. Double heading was a feature of MR expresses. There was some logic behind this, as the MR's routes were more sharply curved than those of the other main line companies, and it was its policy to run lighter, but more frequent, trains. Nevertheless, when one railway writer produced a 'Railway Alphabet' book for younger readers, he wrote:

M is for Midland with engines galore
Two on each train and asking for more

As the century ended, the MR was still expanding. Its partners in Scotland were the Glasgow & South Western Railway and the North British Railway, with the latter helped by the MR contributing thirty per cent of the cost of building the Forth Bridge, opened in 1890. On the other side of Scotland, it acquired a twenty-five per cent stake in the Portpatrick & Wigtownshire Joint Railway, which ran from Castle Douglas to Stranraer and Kirkcudbright, which took traffic that had come off the West Coast line at Dumfries on to connect with the packet service to Larne in Northern Ireland, a route later known as the 'Port Road'. It strengthened its hold on the Ulster market in 1903 when it bought the Belfast & Northern Counties Railway, the most prosperous railway in the north of Ireland. In 1904, it opened a new port at Heysham in Lancashire for packet services to Belfast. It helped to create the Midland & Great Northern Joint Railway in 1893 so that it could reach East Anglia. Less logical, as it was isolated from the rest of its network, was the purchase of the London Tilbury & Southend Railway in 1912, which the MR promised to electrify, but never did. The company did, nevertheless, develop its existing network, separating slow freight trains from fast expresses, so that between London and Leeds it had a higher proportion of quadrupled route mileage than its competitor, the Great Northern.

As a constituent part of the LMS, many of the MR's ideas and practices were adopted, such as central control, but not the legacy of small locomotives.

Chapter 4

The Railways Head for Scotland

The beginning of the nineteenth century marked a major change in the relationship between Scotland and England. Despite the union of the crowns in 1603 when the Scottish James Stuart, or James VI of Scotland, also became James I of England, and the union of the parliaments in 1707, the relationship had been uneasy for most of the eighteenth century, with the French backing the Stuart claim to the throne of Great Britain (Ireland was still to be incorporated to create the United Kingdom). Not all Scots were in favour of the Stuart restoration, especially in the more prosperous cities such as Edinburgh, but elsewhere, especially in the largely Roman Catholic Western Highlands and Western Isles, there was a strong groundswell of support for the Stuarts and even for a return to an independent Scotland.

The Hanoverian monarchs had suppressed dissent, not only by sending in the British Army, whose troops were known as 'redcoats' because of their uniform, but also by placing restrictions on whisky distilling and banning the wearing of tartan.

Nevertheless, the union had shown the Scottish economy to be weaker than that of its southern neighbour, and soon the English pound was worth twenty Scottish pounds. Dual currency notes were issued on both sides of the border.

The nineteenth century marked a sharp change in the relationship between the two countries. In 1837, the new Queen Victoria, just eighteen years old, began her long reign, and one of its distinctive features was the great affection that she and her consort, Prince Albert, felt for Scotland. They had a Highland home at Balmoral, and what might be described as a 'town house' in the Palace of Holyrood House, facing Arthur's Seat on the edge of Edinburgh and just a mile from the fortress of Edinburgh Castle. Royal patronage made Scotland fashionable and marked the start of a growing tourist industry.

Yet it was not just Victoria's support that marked the change. The industrial revolution was based on coal and Scotland was a major source of high-quality coal, much of it from the massive coalfields that surrounded Edinburgh and Glasgow, and which were also to be found in Fife and in Ayrshire. Scottish iron ore was also of high quality, being low in sulphur. Glasgow and all down the Clyde became one of the world's greatest shipbuilding centres. Scotland also had high-quality agricultural produce, and, of course, there were the massive fishing grounds. Long before North Sea oil, Aberdeen was a major fishing port and also the railhead for the extensive agricultural region inland.

The railways made a big difference to the Scottish economy, and eventually they enabled fish and meat from as far north as Aberdeen or Peterhead to reach markets in the south while still in good condition.

Scotland's Railways
At the dawn of the railway age, Scotland had a network of wagon-ways, established in the eighteenth century, to expedite the movement of coal. These depended on horse power, as with similar wagonways elsewhere. Steam first appeared in Scotland in 1817 on the Kilmarnock & Troon Railway, and other mineral lines followed. From 1831, the Garnkirk & Glasgow Railway provided both passenger and freight services using steam power, albeit on a gauge of 4ft 6in, which became known as the 'Scotch Gauge', until standardization throughout Great Britain* later. The GGR claimed to be Scotland's first railway in the accepted sense. Believed to be far busier was the Edinburgh & Dalkeith Railway, opened in 1832 using horse power, but which carried 150,000 passengers in its first year, an incredible figure for the time, although the Forth & Clyde Canal carried 200,000 passengers in 1836.

Nevertheless, as a whole, railway development in Scotland was some time behind that of England, no doubt in part due to the low population density and also the natural barriers, including not only terrain that required extensive tunnels or steep gradients, but also the Tay, the Firth of Forth and further north the Cromarty and Dornoch firths. Perhaps the stately pace of the Forth & Clyde Canal was regarded as sufficient, canals still being seen as an advance on earlier transport, as even the Edinburgh & Glasgow Railway was not

---

*The 4ft 8½in gauge eventually adopted as the standard applied only to England, Scotland and Wales. Throughout Ireland, all of which was then part of the United Kingdom, the standard gauge, also enshrined in legislation, was 5ft 3in. As a result of the high cost of building to this gauge, the country had many narrow gauge lines.

authorized until 1838. The EGR opened in 1842, and carried 200,000 passengers in its first twelve months. This figure had risen to more than a million by 1846.

The border was crossed in three places by 1850, with three routes running via Dumfries and Carstairs in the south-west and Berwick, actually just across the border in England, on the East Coast. The famous Waverley route to Carlisle did not reach the English city until 1862. By this time, the railway had also reached Aberdeen and Inverness was linked by railway to Perth the following year. Extensive local networks grew up not only around Edinburgh and Glasgow, but also at Dundee.

Yet it was still an incomplete network, broken by the Tay and the Forth. Through services were available, with passengers transferring to ferries, and the world's first train ferry operated for goods wagons between Granton and Burntisland from 1850. The vast indentations made by the Forth and the Tay estuaries mainly affected the East Coast group of companies and especially the North British Railway, whose territory it was, giving the West Coast group of companies an advantage until the estuaries could be bridged.

While there was only one route from Edinburgh to Aberdeen or to Inverness, between Edinburgh and Glasgow, the two largest cities, several routes were built. Four remain in use today.

For internal services, Scotland did, nevertheless, fare far better than Wales, which had to accept that the main traffic flows were east-west, with North Wales looking to Manchester, Chester and Crewe for its railway routings, mid-Wales to Birmingham and the Midlands, and South Wales initially to Gloucester until the Severn Tunnel was built, when the route passing Bristol became the most obvious. To travel by train from North Wales to South Wales, including the capital, Cardiff, it was necessary to cross briefly into England. In Scotland, however, the route from the north to England was always via either Edinburgh or Glasgow.

Across the Border

While the early railways had been promoted to meet local needs, it was not long before the major trunk routes began to be built. In 1838, Paddington and Euston both appeared in London to serve the trunk railway ambitions of the Great Western Railway and the London & Birmingham Railway respectively. Scotland, was, of course, a far more difficult target because of the distance involved, and so it was natural that it should be reached by lines that had set out to link London with Birmingham and Manchester, or York and then Newcastle. These centres served to boost the traffic potential of the lines, and not only between them and London, as reasonable traffic flows were also developed northwards. The difference was, of course, that the railway lines that developed on the West Coast did not run through Birmingham and Manchester to Scotland, avoiding both cities, although on the East Coast they did run through York and Newcastle. One thing that both the East Coast Main Line and the West Coast Main Line did have in common was that both required collaboration between companies, with the WCML being a partnership between the London & North Western Railway, as the London & Birmingham became, and the Caledonian Railway, while the ECML required the Great Northern, the North Eastern and the North British Railway to work together. Even so, in the latter case, the North Eastern insisted that its locomotives haul trains as far as Edinburgh, even though north of Newcastle was North British territory.

The first through services were on the West Coast, completed in 1858, with Euston as the London terminus. The East Coast service from King's Cross followed in 1862. Between 1850 and 1860, the 'Scotch Railways Agreement' determined that Glasgow could only be served from Euston and Edinburgh could only be served from King's Cross. Further agreements meant that the combined revenues were apportioned. There was competition, but speed was not a factor at first, even though from 1862 the main ECML day train reached Edinburgh an hour faster than the best train to Glasgow: the LNWR did not see any merit in high speed as it consumed too much coal. Until 1887, the fastest East Coast trains did not allow second or third-class passengers.

In 1875–76, the Midland Railway opened its seventy-two-mile route between Settle and Carlisle with the intention of becoming the third route between London and Scotland. The LNWR, which had earlier refused to collaborate with the Midland, relented and, in an attempt to persuade the MR that the new route was unnecessary, agreed to collaborate. The Midland was tempted, but its new route was also supported by the Lancashire & Yorkshire Railway and the North British, as well as its main partner in Scotland, the Glasgow & South Western Railway, a competitor of the Caledonian, and these companies insisted that the project went ahead.

This new competitor disturbed the cosy relationship between the East and West Coast groups. One reason for the LNWR's change of heart was the realization that this was a competitor that could not be influenced. The MR's opening shot was one that was to have profound implications for all of Britain's railways in the years that followed, although it was to take ten years before another railway copied the Midland. On 1 January 1875, the Midland Railway abolished second-class fares and scrapped its small stock of third-class carriages. A third-class fare now admitted the less well-off passengers to significantly more comfortable accommodation, marking the single most important advance in passenger well-being since the 'Cheap Trains Act' of 1844, which led to the Parliamentary trains, charging a fare of no more than a penny a mile, providing enclosed accommodation for all passengers and stopping at all stations on the line, with at least one service a day, including Sundays. The Midland pressed home this advantage by reducing first-class fares, so that despite its longer route, it was also the cheapest route between London and Scotland.

Even before this, the MR knew that its advantage lay in the superior comfort of its trains, so that while its route to Scotland could not be the fastest, it would be the most comfortable. The MR also had a superior finish to its trains, with up to seventeen coats of paint on a carriage. Its one weakness was that it favoured small locomotives, partly because many of its routes had extensive curves, such that even by the end of the nineteenth century the Midland was using 4–4–0s rather than the 4–6–0s that were becoming popular, and did not favour the 4–6–2 Pacific at all. The downside was, of course, that many trains had to be double-headed, requiring four footplate crew rather than two.

It is worth mentioning here that even before the arrival of Pullman carriages with dining at the passengers' seats and often just one seat on each side of the aisle, and sleeping cars, which were initially limited to first-class passengers and which, like the Pullmans, attracted a supplement on top of the usual fare, there were many classes on some railways. The Parliamentary trains had led many railway companies to create a fourth class, largely to protect their third-class revenue, while there were others that charged supplements for first and second-class travel. All together, some have identified as many as seven classes on some of Britain's railways.

With three groups of companies competing for the valuable Anglo-Scottish passenger market, it was inevitable that sooner or later speed would become an important element.

The Routes

As already mentioned, the Midland Railway had the longest of the three main routes between London and Scotland, and it was also one with many tight curves, so all in all it could not be the fastest. The other two routes were not easy working, especially in the days of steam.

Travel between Euston and Glasgow or Edinburgh was notorious for the steep summits of Shap, in what is now Cumbria, and Beattock, just north of the border in Scotland. What made these two so difficult was that between them the line fell down to sea level at Carlisle, so travelling in either direction the train was faced with a steep ascent, a steep descent, a call at Carlisle for an engine change, or at least a footplate crew change, then another steep ascent and descent.

The journey to and from King's Cross saw difficult gradients north of Berwick-on-Tweed, especially around Cockburn's Path.

All three routes had difficult down exits from London, caused not only by rising ground, but also by the need to dive under the Regent's Canal. Indeed, at first the LNWR had its trains worked up from Euston through a tunnel by rope haulage using a stationary steam engine. This didn't last long as traction improved.

While never rope-worked, the exit from King's Cross was, if anything, more difficult. There was very little open line between the end of the platforms and the first tunnel. Indeed, long trains could have the locomotive sitting in the first tunnel, known now as Gasworks Tunnel but at the time named Maiden Lane Tunnel. The track, claimed on many gradient charts to be level to the mouth of the tunnel, in fact dips down at 1:79 into the tunnel and then rises towards the daylight at the northern end. The dip took the line under the Regent's Canal, and was often useful as it enabled the locomotive to get a grip before beginning the long ascent of Holloway Bank.

Heading north, the locomotives would steam through the open between Maiden Lane or Gasworks Tunnel and Copenhagen Tunnel, through a short open stretch known as Belle Isle, a section in steep-sided cutting that barely allowed steam and smoke to escape. The average gradient through both tunnels was 1:107.

Inevitably, the rails would be slippery, and not just on wet days, as the high volumes of steam from hard-working locomotives in such confined spaces meant that there was much moisture around.

Once free of the first two tunnels, there were five more before the locomotive reached Potters Bar, just over twelve and a half miles from King's Cross.

Chapter 5

The Age of Competition

The early railways are often seen as providing intense competition between the companies. This is only partly true. There was intense competition where companies abutted one another or operated between the same two cities, but for the most part they were seen as local monopolies, and they in fact became much less local as time passed and amalgamations or agreements on collaboration came into being.

An example of how extreme competition could be arose on services between London and Portsmouth. Until'the London & South Western Line was extended from Godalming, just south of Guildford, in 1858, the LSWR approached Portsmouth via Eastleigh and Fareham. The rival London Brighton & South Coast Railway approached first via Brighton and then from Arundel. The 'shorter' and more direct Arundel route was eighty-five miles, but the line via Guildford was a touch over seventy-four miles. Neither route was perfect. The Arundel route ran across relatively low-lying and marshy land, with rivers, and the Guildford line had some considerable gradients as well as cuttings, which could fill with snow, and embankments.

When the direct line through to Portsmouth was completed, the first train sent down it was not a regular passenger service, but a special train, packed with workmen. This was not to test the track and signals, as that had been done before the line was allowed to open by the Board of Trade. Approaching Havant, the LSWR train found that the LBSCR had chained a locomotive to the tracks, and when the workmen alighted from the LSWR train to clear the obstruction, the 'Battle of Havant' began.

The LSWR eventually won and started its service between London Waterloo and Portsmouth. The two railway companies were allowed to extend their lines through to Portsmouth Harbour station, ideal for the ferries to Ryde on the Isle of Wight and convenient for the steam launch service across Portsmouth Harbour to Gosport, and, of course, convenient for the Royal Dockyard, the existence of which had been the Admiralty's reason for trying to bar railway access to the harbour in the first place!

Sanity prevailed in the end. The line from Havant to Portsmouth Harbour, and a branch to Southsea, was operated jointly by the two companies. Moreover, they also jointly operated the Portsmouth–Ryde passenger ferry and, which really is astonishing, the line from Ryde Pierhead through Ryde Esplanade to Smallbrook Junction, just beyond Ryde St John's Road station. Smallbrook Junction marked the division of the Isle of Wight Railway's line from Ryde to Ventnor from that of the Isle of Wight Central Railway from Ryde to Newport and Cowes. Neither the LSWR nor the LBSCR ran trains on the Isle of Wight.

This was a clear example of two monopolies competing where they joined over traffic to one major city, Portsmouth, with the competition not only commercial, but also violent. Collaboration also meant a confirmation of both monopolies. The eventual outcome was, however, the only logical way of solving the problem.

There was also competition between the London Chatham & Dover Railway and the South Eastern Railway between London and Dover, the main port for France and Belgium. The LCDR had come into being as a result of anger and disappointment in the Medway towns over the SER's route, which ran south through Ashford and Folkestone. The trouble was that the available traffic was insufficient for two railway companies and they eventually pauperized each other. Once again sanity prevailed in collaboration, with the two companies, while remaining nominally independent and separately quoted on the stock market, becoming the South East & Chatham Railway, with the SECR effectively being the management committee.

Longer-Distance Competition

Not all of the competition was between companies in the south of England. The London & South Western Railway was an active competitor in the traffic between London and Plymouth, but on this occasion its rival was the Great Western Railway. Plymouth was then, as now, an important naval base, but the real driver for competition was what the railways would call 'boat train traffic'. This meant passengers being dropped off or boarding transatlantic liners at Plymouth, so saving up to two days on their journey to or from London in the days when the capital was the port for long-distance liner voyages and before Southampton was developed (by the Southern Railway) to take over this role.

Even after belatedly being granted powers to operate shipping, railway management was always decidedly land-lubberish. There was no such thing as a ship, no matter how large: ships were always 'boats'.

The LSWR was competitive in this market until the GWR introduced a 'cut-off', shortening its line between London, Exeter and Plymouth in 1906. When the competition first started in 1862, after the LSWR accelerated its service between London and Exeter, the GWR route meant running over the Bristol & Exeter Railway, and the two companies responded by improving the timings for their best train. This was the first railway race. The racing on this route was ended in 1906 both by the GWR's cut-off, which gave the company a shorter distance than the LSWR route, but also by an accident at Salisbury on the LSWR on 30 June. An up express from Plymouth had a locomotive change at Templecombe, after which the driver attempted to run through Salisbury station at high speed, ignoring the permanent way slack, or speed limit, which was necessary as the station had sharp curves at both ends. The entire train was derailed and of forty-three passengers, twenty-three were killed.

The lines between London and Scotland which concern us also had a chequered history as regards competition. Between 1860 and 1870, the 'Scotch Railways Agreement' meant that Edinburgh was only served from King's Cross and Glasgow only served from Euston. This was followed by a period of pooled receipts, until the Midland intervened, as we will see later.

While this book is about the races to the north and over the border into Scotland at a time when both the East and West Coast companies could serve both Edinburgh and Glasgow, and then Aberdeen as well, there were many other cities on the way that enjoyed two or even three routes to and from London. These were often more exciting than the Anglo-Scottish routes, on which competition was initially muted due to pooling agreements, until the Midland Railway entered the fray.

Birmingham, Manchester and Sheffield were amongst the cities where there was keen competition between companies to provide the best timings to and from London. Birmingham was served by the Great Western from Paddington and the London & North Western from Euston. Manchester was served by the London & North Western and by an alliance of the Manchester Sheffield & Lincoln and the Great Northern, operating from King's Cross until, at the end of the century, the MSLR became the Great Central and had its own route into London's Marylebone. Sheffield was served by both the MSLR and the Midland.

There were other routes on which competition existed; sometimes convenience was a greater incentive than speed. There were many who saw the competition as being wasteful, and indeed it is hard to argue against that. In 1888 there were three expresses from London to Manchester at 2.00pm, leaving London termini less than a mile apart.

Competition was not profitable. Many railway companies had chairmen whose ambitions outstripped commercial reality. Watkin was a case in point. His Manchester Sheffield & Lincoln, or MSL, was known as 'money sunk and lost'. When it allowed its ambitions full reign and extended into London with the opening of Marylebone, it celebrated by adopting a new name, the Great Central, or GC, which to the cynics was known as 'gone completely', referring to their investment! This was at a time, in the Edwardian era and before the First World War, when many railways were at their most profitable.

Other routes on which competition existed included London to Cambridge, with services by the Great Northern from King's Cross and from Liverpool Street by the Great Eastern, and, of course, between London and Southend-on-Sea, served by the Great Eastern from Liverpool Street and the London Tilbury & Southend from Fenchurch Street. Grouping did little to resolve matters, as the Midland had acquired the LTSR, so that became part of the LMS, while the GE passed into the LNER.

Elsewhere, there was competition between Edinburgh and Glasgow and across the Pennines.

The years immediately before the turn of the century were less good. Between 1894 and 1895, receipts per route mile fell from £2,880 to £2,834 on the London & North Western; from £2,763 to £2,719 on the Great Northern; and from £2,988 to £2,895 on the Midland. Both the last two companies saw receipts per train mile also fall, but the LNWR enjoyed an improvement from 5s 4¾d to 5s 5¼d.

Competition or Coordination

It is often assumed that the Victorian era was one of free enterprise and competition. This is not quite right. The Victorian era saw the first nationalization, that of the telegraph system, which brought together a fragmented system and created a viable nationwide network. It was a great success because, unlike the railways, there was no such thing as through running over another company's cables as there was over tracks. Many of the systems taken over actually belonged to the railway companies, and the price paid was at the very least useful to the weaker companies. For example, the London Chatham & Dover Railway, at the time actually in receivership, used the £100,000 (around £5 million today) paid by the Post Office for its telegraph system towards the building of a much-needed new station in the City of London at Holborn Viaduct. In fact, the age saw a move away from the idea of the state providing a service, such as the Royal Mail, towards the acquisition by the state of a functioning business or businesses.

Because the railways were often seen as having a monopoly, at least locally, despite the multitude of companies, some compared the iron road with the public highway, especially when at first many railways were meant to be open to anyone who wanted to run a train, and so the railways also brought into being the concept of nationalization, and the concept actually pre-dated the start of the Victoria era in 1837.

As early as 1836, one James Morrison wanted Parliament to revise the railway's tolls, this being the time when railways were seen as being rather like turnpike trusts, with open access to anyone who wanted to put a carriage or wagon on the iron road. Greater state control of the railways had been proposed almost from the dawn of the railway age by those who were concerned about the impact of the new form of transport. No less a person than the Duke of Wellington, in opposition in 1834, had urged Lord Melbourne to protect the country against the mismanagement and monopoly of the railways. This, of course, shows an early divergence of opinion between those who saw the railways as a monopoly supplier and those who felt that the monopoly was nothing more than the superiority of the railways compared with all other forms of inland transport. Certainly, throughout the early years, Parliament never intended any one railway to have a monopoly.

Outright proposals for nationalization appeared as early as 1843, when a certain William Galt wrote a series of four books, in 1843 and 1844, on *Railway Reform*, and it was this that led Gladstone to include in his Railway Regulation Act 1844 a measure giving the government the power to acquire, from 1865 onwards, any company sanctioned following the 1844 Act. Galt was a solicitor and it is generally taken that in pressing for reform of the railways, he was more concerned with what would be best for the country as a whole, seeing the railways as similar to the highways and the Post Office, than advocating state ownership as part of a political platform. He returned to his theme in 1864 when his book was revised and republished, providing a thorough survey of the state of the nation's railways at the time, and then went on to appear before the Royal Commission on the Railways the following year. The members of the Devon Commission certainly considered nationalization, but decided that nothing further should be done.

Walter Bagehot was another advocate of nationalization, writing in *The Economist*: 'It is easy to show that the transfer of the railways to the state would be very beneficial, if only it can be effected.' He was unsure about just how it could be done. Advocates of nationalization fell into several camps, and it was not until much later that this became part of a political platform, and one that contemplated state ownership far in excess of the railways. Many of the earlier advocates saw the railways as constituting a public service, rather like the Royal Mail. It is not surprising, therefore, that Sir Rowland Hill, the Postmaster-General, was amongst those keen on nationalizing the railways, although it is more surprising to find that he was joined by, for example, a shipowner who was also a director of the London & North Western Railway. The Board of Trade inspector, Henry Tyler, was also pro-nationalization, although this did not stop him from later becoming a director of the Grand Trunk Railway of Canada and a Conservative MP.

Arguments against nationalization largely centred on the powers of patronage that it would put in the hands of politicians, as it was alleged had been the case in Belgium. The problem was, of course, that state ownership of the telegraph system was an almost instant success. This strengthened the argument of those advocating similar treatment for the railways. On the other hand, a railway is not a telegraph system. Inter-operability is far easier to ensure between railways even within different ownership, and there are opportunities for competition that can benefit the consumer and even hasten technical progress. It is also true that the railways could not guarantee that their predominant position in inland transport would last forever, and even the future shape of the railway network was unclear. Once again, though, we come back to another argument, which is that the railway network would have been far sparser were it not for the boom of speculation. The lines in the far north of Scotland were built with public money or relief from rates, and it would seem fair to speculate that had the railways been nationalized earlier, many uneconomic lines might have been built for social and strategic purposes, while the development of lines in the heavily industrialized and densely-populated areas might have been relatively neglected. One can surmise that there would have been too few lines, with many cross-country routes not built and the trunk network having fewer sections with multiple track (i.e. more than two lines). The state of Britain's motorway network gives us a clue.

Nationalization finally became a political issue in 1894, when the Amalgamated Society of Railway Servants, the predecessor of the National Union of Railwaymen, declared in favour of state ownership. In 1899, Sir George Findlay, a director of the London & North Western Railway, looked at the problem and, while opposed to nationalization, worked out a system which could allow it to work. The new Labour Party made nationalization one of its core policies early in the twentieth century.

Many advocates of nationalization saw the railways becoming a department of state, and one wonders just how many, especially in the trade unions, would have been so keen had they realized that it would eventually be state ownership at arm's length, in what would effectively be a state corporation.

A further Royal Commission was appointed in 1913 by the then Liberal government to consider the question of nationalization of the railways, but its deliberations were overtaken by the outbreak of the First World War. Wartime saw the railways under state control, and in 1919 the question of nationalization was raised again, but instead it was decided to amalgamate the railway companies into four strong geographically-based groups. This move might well have been the result of the country's parlous public finances at the time, but it could also have been part of the first signs of political interference in business, as these were the days when the chemical and electrical industries were rationalized, with the formation of Imperial Chemical Industries (ICI), and Amalgamated Electrical Industries (AEI).

After a further spell of government control during the Second World War, the post-war Labour administration felt that it had a mandate for nationalization, although, as a rear-guard action, some directors of the London & North Eastern Railway, one of the grouped companies, tried to plan a system that would transfer the infrastructure to the state, but allow the companies to remain as managers (not so different from the situation today), but this was rejected.

Chapter 6

Barriers to Progress

A quick look at a map of the British Isles will show that the eastern coastline of Scotland is heavily indented, with the massive firths or wide estuaries of both the Forth and of the Tay. These were the most obvious obstacles to trains, but far from the only ones. The River Tyne also had to be bridged in the east, and the Solway in the west. The Pennines effectively kept the East and West Coast lines apart, but the sparsely-populated Scottish borders were also an expensive obstacle, and it is worth noting that, even today, the main line from Edinburgh to London does not swing south immediately it leaves the Scottish capital, but instead initially runs eastwards.

In fact the railway routes are the result of compromise, for even the ambitious Victorian engineers, not easily daunted, had to take into account the topography of the country through which they worked. A straight line from London to Edinburgh would run very close to Sheffield and Bradford, not through York or Newcastle. The line chosen runs through both York and Newcastle, but both cities at one stage had termini where trains continuing south or north had to reverse, which was hardly conducive to high-speed running. Between Newcastle and Edinburgh steep gradients existed, especially for northbound trains.

The line from London to Glasgow was straighter, but the main city in the north of England was Carlisle, lying almost at sea level, but with the steep gradients of Shap to the south and Beattock to the north.

The importance of bridging the Tay and the Forth was that, once completed, the through railway line meant that the East Coast Main Line became the faster and shorter option for passengers from London to Dundee and Aberdeen, Scotland's fourth- and third-largest cities respectively.

The newest of the routes linking London with Scotland, the Midland route, was curved and longer and the company did not involve itself in the races. That it was not short of engineering challenges can be seen by the mighty yet elegant Ribblehead viaduct on the Selby and Carlisle line.

Running Through the Cities

In 1844, for Newcastle it was a case of being so close, yet so far, from a through line. The Great North of England and the Newcastle & Darlington Junction Railways provided a through line to York and London from Gateshead, but could not bridge the Tyne because of the depth of the gorge. It was not until George Hudson agreed to provide a double-deck bridge carrying trains on the upper level and wagons below that a bridge could be built by Robert Stephenson, completed in 1849 at the then astronomical cost of £500,000. The following year Newcastle Central was opened. A line between Gateshead and Carlisle had opened as early as 1837. For a while the NER had a monopoly on railway services in and around Tyneside, but this was broken in 1864 when the Blyth & Tyne Railway entered the city, with its terminus at Picton House. However, the port of Blyth did not fulfil its promise and in 1874 the BTR was purchased by the NER. During the railway races Newcastle was to prove a hindrance for the East Coast competitors, as it was not until the opening of the King Edward VII Bridge, west of Stephenson's high-level bridge, in 1906, that trains running through to and from Scotland were spared the time-consuming reversal at Central.

York's bottleneck was removed by the time of the first races. Like Newcastle, York was on the railway map at an early stage, as during the 1830s it had first the York & North Midland Railway and then the Great North of England Railway, so that the city had lines radiating from it to London, Leeds and Hull, while local lines followed, linking the city to Scarborough, Harrogate, Market Weighton and Beverley. By 1850 there was a line northwards to Edinburgh. These lines were promoted by the controversial railway promoter George Hudson, whose activities benefited York most of all, and made the city the most important railway junction between Newcastle and London. His influence was such that the railway was able to site its station actually inside the ancient and confined city, even to the extent of breaching the city walls. By 1854, the North Eastern Railway had a monopoly, but another seven railway companies had running powers into York. New lines to the south were built twice to reduce mileage, while the station eventually had to be rebuilt outside the city walls to ensure that enough space was available for the growing demand and to avoid the need for trains to reverse. The new station opened in 1877 and eventually had sixteen platforms, but was built on a sharp curve.

Although one of the obstacles on the East Coast was thus removed eleven years before the first races, at the time the lack of water troughs on the East Coast line meant that trains still had to call at York to change locomotives. The West Coast route, in contrast, already possessed this time-saving feature.

Across the Tay
The North British Railway's route through the east of Scotland was punctuated by the wide estuaries or 'firths' of the rivers Forth and Tay, across which the company ran train ferries. This delayed through services north of Edinburgh and the crossings were often stormy and uncomfortable. Anxious to beat the Caledonian Railway for traffic to Perth, Dundee and Aberdeen, the North British commissioned a bridge across the Tay from the north coast of Fife to Dundee, designed and built by Thomas Bouch. The bridge opened to traffic on 31 May 1878, and during summer 1879 HM Queen Victoria travelled by train across the bridge to bestow a knighthood on Bouch. Logic would have suggested that the Forth be bridged first, but this did not happen and, with hindsight, that was probably fortunate, especially as, until the Tay Bridge disaster, Bouch's design for the Forth Bridge was the favourite.

On the night of Sunday 28 December 1879, the East Coast of Scotland was battered by a heavy storm, sometimes referred to as a hurricane, an extremely rare event in the British Isles. The wind gusted and there were heavy showers of sleet throughout the evening. The 4.30pm from Edinburgh to Dundee had crossed the Firth of Forth on the train ferry between Granton, now effectively part of Edinburgh, to Burntisland in Fife, which it left at 6.30pm before journeying onwards, stopping at Leuchars, followed by the rural halt at St Fort. The train was not very busy, with around seventy-three passengers aboard, as well as the three-man crew of driver, fireman and guard, but the first-class compartments were empty. It was running slightly late, about four minutes, and no doubt the driver was planning to use the crossing of the Firth of Tay to make up some of the lost time. At 7.13pm, the driver slowed the train to pick up the single-line working token at the cabin on the south side of what was at the time the world's longest railway bridge.

The storm was getting worse, and not only had blown down a chimney at Dundee Tay Bridge Station, smashing the station's glass roof, but had also managed to blow loaded coal wagons back along a siding running from the bridge to the goods yard.

By this time the train had steamed onto the bridge, but it is believed that a third-class carriage derailed, and was then stopped when it hit a girder tie-bar. The heavy guard's van immediately behind it then rode over it, crushing the occupants, and the vibration caused cast iron columns under the bridge deck to fracture and collapse. In less than a minute, the bridge was collapsing and the train fell into the storm-tossed tidal estuary below. The force of the fall was such that many of those aboard suffered fractured limbs, but this was of academic interest only, as those who had survived the derailment and accident on the rails above were all drowned.

The alarm was raised by James Smith, the stationmaster at Dundee Tay Bridge. At 7.23pm, concerned that the train had not arrived, he attempted to telegraph the cabin on the south side of the bridge, and was alarmed to find that he could not get a reply. Initially suspecting a locomotive failure, he started out with the locomotive superintendent, James Roberts. They soon met people who reported seeing the bridge fall into the firth, but continued until they could see for themselves, upon which sight the stationmaster went back to the station to close the entrances and evacuate the crowd of people waiting for the train, mainly for their safety, as glass from the roof was still falling onto the platform. Roberts continued out onto the bridge and was the first person to discover the full extent of the disaster, crawling out with great difficulty in the high winds until he came to the railway lines trailing into the water far below.

In fact, no one at Dundee knew whether the train had been on the bridge or whether it was still on its way from Burntisland. Smith telegraphed the North British Railway company's headquarters in Edinburgh and then chartered a steamer.

At the subsequent enquiry, the designer, Sir Thomas Bouch, soon became the culprit, but the bridge failed not only because of weaknesses in its design, parts of which were untried, but also because of poor workmanship and supervision, and because the Perth Harbour Commissioners, some miles further upstream, had insisted that the bridge be high enough to allow large sailing vessels to pass under it.

The irony was that the year 1879 could have been one of the century's best for railway safety, as the total, including those lost in the disaster, was seventy-five fatalities. Safety standards at the time, including the wooden structure of most railway carriages and the risk of fire from oil or gas lamps after a collision or derailment, was such that a single accident could distort the figures, as in 1889 when eighty-eight passengers were killed, eighty of them in the Armagh disaster in Northern Ireland. The best year was 1891, with five passengers killed, followed by 1885 with six and 1886 with eight. While 1889 was the worst, there were eighty-six deaths amongst passengers in 1874. The combined total for the years 1874, 1875, 1876, 1878 and 1889 was well over a thousand, 262 of which were victims at Armagh in 1889. Needless to say, there were no injured passengers in the Tay Bridge disaster.

William Barlow built a more substantial replacement bridge that opened in 1887. The piers and other remains of the original bridge were demolished as a condition for authorization for the new bridge, but the base of the piers can still be seen upstream of the existing bridge.

Across the Forth

Bouch was disgraced and the appalling circumstances no doubt contributed to his early death. His plans for a bridge over the Forth, a form of suspension bridge, were scrapped and the work given elsewhere.

Usually simply referred to as the 'Forth Bridge', the bridge was needed to enable trains from the south to run through to Dundee and Aberdeen, replacing the train ferry introduced in 1850. Throughout the 1860s and 1870s, a succession of proposals were made for bridges across the Firth of Forth, and it was not until 1878 that William Arrol started work on Bouch's stiffened suspension bridge. Work stopped immediately after the Tay Bridge disaster in 1879, although Bouch's Forth Bridge was not officially abandoned until 1881.

With Bouch discredited, it was not until 1881 that Sir John Fowler and Benjamin Baker were commissioned to build their design, consisting of three double cantilevers with suspended spans in between. This design was refined into the present bridge, with main spans of 1,700ft, which at the time made it the greatest bridge in the world. In reacting to the Tay disaster, the new bridge was designed to resist a wind force of 56lbs per square foot, and is widely regarded as being over-cautious in design, but today it can safely accommodate trains many times heavier than those running at the time it was completed. William Arrol remained as contractor.

With the North British Railway crippled by the loss of the Tay Bridge, it was joined by the Great Northern, North Eastern and Midland Railways as joint shareholders in the Forth Bridge Company. The NBR worked the trains once the project was completed in 1890, but only north of Edinburgh, as the NER insisted that it should work the section of the line from York to Edinburgh over the NBR's rails between Newcastle and the Scottish capital. This was a wise decision, as the NER had the more powerful locomotives, but was very much against the NBR's wishes, showing that on the Victorian railway, even collaborative ventures were not without friction.

Famous for many years for the team of painters who had to start repainting the bridge whenever they had just finished, in recent years more modern paint technology has been applied. Work ended in 2011 with the promise that no further painting would be necessary for twenty years.

The Impact of the Bridges

The bridges changed the railway map and timetables dramatically. Before they were built, the fastest railway route to Aberdeen from London was that of the West Coast companies, even though as the crow flies the East Coast route was far shorter.

Once over the Tay Bridge, the two routes converged on Kinnaber Junction. While the 1895 race was to Aberdeen, rather than to Edinburgh or Glasgow as in 1888, in reality the race was to Kinnaber Junction, as the first train to reach it was already the victor.

Chapter 7

The First Races

Discussing the bridges that were so important to the East Coast Main Line is, of course, to jump ahead, as the first races between London and Scotland pre-dated the opening of the Forth Bridge. Even had the first Tay Bridge not collapsed in 1879, it would not have played an important role, as the races would still have been to Edinburgh, not Aberdeen, as the East Coast companies would still have been burdened with the train ferry across the Forth, ruling out any prospect of a race to Aberdeen in 1888.

Even before it abolished second-class fares and started to scrap its third-class carriages, the Midland Railway caused a stir amongst the railway community in March 1872 when it announced that from 1 April it would provide third-class accommodation on all of its trains. It was the first company to do so, as previously the fastest trains had offered first and second-class accommodation only, although the Great Northern had third-class carriages on certain trains that were directly in competition with the Midland (once that company's extension to St Pancras had opened in 1868). The crack 'Special Scotch Express', as the 10.00am departure from King's Cross was named (it later became the 'Flying Scotsman'), was at the time first and second-class only.

The GNR's reaction was twofold. First, it accelerated the daily 10.00am departure in each direction from King's Cross and Edinburgh Waverley by an hour, and second, while this prestigious train retained its exclusive first and second-class carriages, a second train was provided at 10.10am with accommodation for all three classes of passenger, running to the pre-acceleration timings. The accelerated schedule was most marked for travellers between London and York, which under the new schedule took just four hours fifteen minutes, giving an average speed of 44mph, but north of York the improvement was not so great, taking four hours fifty minutes to reach Edinburgh. At this time, the call at York was necessary as it provided a twenty-five-minute interval for lunch. This meant that the journey between the two capital cities still took more than nine hours, although this was definitely an improvement on the earlier timing of almost eleven hours end-to-end.

The GNR and its associate on the East Coast Main Line, the North-Eastern, knew that the 'Flying Scotsman' itself was not at risk from the Midland Railway, but the situation would change once the MR completed its route from Selby to Carlisle. Although the express ran over North British tracks to reach Waverley, it was worked from York to Edinburgh by NER locomotives. The NBR was known to be hedging its bets and it seemed likely that once the Midland route to Scotland was completed, an Edinburgh service would be provided by the Midland in collaboration with the NBR. In short, the GNR and NER were attempting to establish a reputation for high speed and high-quality service in advance of the competition.

Interestingly, in the light of what was to follow, the West Coast companies made no attempt to match the East Coast timings. One reason could be that the leading company, the London & North Western Railway, had a frugal approach to railway operation, and objected to ever higher speeds on the grounds that they increased coal consumption. Senior officers were told to resist any attempts at acceleration in their dealings with other companies. Economy was practised to the extent that the gas lamps at Euston on the arrival platform were dimmed and only turned up as an express arrived.

Conversely, the LNWR was in effect what would be known today as the 'market leader' for third-class traffic.

The Midland Shows its Hand
Derby was not finished and had a further surprise waiting for its competitors. On 7 October 1874, the Midland announced that, from 1 January 1875, second-class would be abolished and the small stock of third-class carriages disposed of, while first-class fares would be reduced to the second-class rate, then 1½d per mile. This was the single biggest improvement in the welfare of the third-class passenger since the introduction of the Parliamentary trains some thirty years earlier.

Having earlier pooled their receipts, the state of competition between the East and West Coast companies had been limited. The aggressive approach of their new competitor provoked uproar. The companies objected strongly both to the abolition of second-class and especially to the reduction in first-class fares, and demanded that the

Midland should withdraw its planned fares cut. They also insisted that no railway company should take such drastic action without first calling a special conference. The Midland, faced with a longer route than either of the existing routes between London and Scotland, was relying on the excellence of its carriages and the reduced fares to attract passengers and remain competitive.

The Midland stood its ground and there were no sanctions available to the other companies that could force it to rescind the fares cut, which gave the Midland the lowest first-class fare on the Anglo-Scottish routes. The other companies bowed to the inevitable and reduced their first-class fares to the Midland level to remain competitive, but retained second class. The GNR and NER did not allow third-class passengers to use the 'Flying Scotsman'. Anticipating that the Settle and Carlisle line would be opened in 1876, that summer's time-table saw a further thirty minutes cut from the schedule of the 'Flying Scotsman'. Faced with this, at last the LNWR reduced the through journey time off its 10.00am Scotch express from Euston, cutting ten minutes off the run to Carlisle so that it took seven and a half hours, an average speed of 39.8mph. True to form, however, the LNWR did not actually accelerate the running of the train, which would have demanded more coal, but cut the thirty minutes allowed for lunch at Preston to twenty minutes.

For many years, even after the advent of the dining car, many railway hotels offered luncheon baskets to departing travellers. This was an attractive proposition, albeit an expensive one, as it meant that the brief time allotted for the luncheon break could be spent relieving oneself and stretching legs cramped from spending so long in a railway compartment without a corridor for the restless to patrol. Getting and eating a meal at Preston or York was not for the meek and mild, as one had to elbow one's way to the head of the queue and be prepared to gobble the victuals provided quickly enough to be able to take a drink and perform other necessary bodily functions. It was all the worse for the fact that someone at the LNWR had considered it a bright idea that the arrival of the northbound and southbound expresses should be coordinated so that they arrived at the same time and everyone could be fed at once. Easing the pressure by having an interval between the arrivals was definitely not considered. Doubtless sales of luncheon hampers at Euston and Carlisle, or even Glasgow, soared after the luncheon interval was reduced!

Competition that should have ensured a sparkling service had varied results: comfort from the Midland, speed from the Great Northern and parsimony from the London & North Western.

Of course, if one chose the Midland service, operated jointly with the North British, for some fortunate passengers the choice between a luncheon hamper and a hastily gobbled meal of dubious quality was unnecessary, as the Midland soon introduced Pullman cars, bought from the United States, with meals and other refreshments served to first-class passengers at their seats in return for a Pullman surcharge. This was an expensive, but comfortable and civilized, means of travelling long distances.

London and Edinburgh

The route that was most sensitive to competition was that between London and Edinburgh, over which the East and West Coast groups were most evenly matched. The through speeds, end-to-end including stops, did not top 50mph. The Great Northern came closest with a run from Grantham to York at 49.6mph, or 100 minutes for the 82.7 miles. The crack 10.00am departure from King's Cross, the 'Special Scotch Express', later known as 'The Flying Scotsman', reached Edinburgh at 7.00pm, or after nine hours, and was restricted to first and second-class passengers only. It was followed by a train open to all three classes which left at 10.10am, a hangover from the accelerations of 1876, and reached Edinburgh at 8.10pm, taking ten hours. The West Coast had just a 10.00am departure from Euston, which reached Edinburgh at 8.00pm, also taking ten hours and open to all three classes. Despite its longer route, the Midland and North British service was competitive on these timings, leaving St Pancras at 10.35am and reaching Edinburgh at 8.42pm. It carried only first and third-class passengers, as there was no longer any second class on the Midland.

The opening shot in this battle between the railway companies was in fact fired in 1887, when the London & North Western Railway finally accelerated its 10.00am departure so that the train arrived at both Edinburgh and Glasgow, having divided at Carlisle, at 7.45pm. The LNWR contributed ten minutes to this saving in time, cutting four minutes off the timing between Rugby and Crewe, having cut a further two minutes off the call at Rugby, a further minute off the run from Crewe to Preston, and a further three minutes between Preston and Carlisle. Despite this, the run between Rugby and Crewe was at an average speed of just 47.7mph.

This was the summer schedule, which at least one railway historian links to Queen Victoria bestowing a baronetcy on the LNWR's chairman, Richard Moon. It was certainly a significant concession from a man who insisted on running express trains at 40mph and who believed, in the face of all evidence to the contrary, that speed provided no commercial advantage. To be fair, the LNWR had a good reputation for punctuality, and running at well below the maximum speed of the express locomotives meant that timetables were more robust and drivers could make up time lost. The there was also the question of comfort. Suspension systems were not as sophisticated as today and track was jointed rather than welded, so high-speed running could be uncomfortable, even though here again the LNWR had a well-deserved reputation for the quality of its track and was amongst the first to employ lengths of rail 60ft long.

There is another aspect to the question of speed that is probably lost on most of us today. Railways today are expected to be high speed to woo passengers away from the airlines, especially on domestic routes, but in Europe higher speeds also mean competition with cross-border air services. The Eurostar trains linking London with Paris have been successful in this, after an uncertain beginning, so that there are far fewer flights between the two capitals than there used to be. During the period of the races, travellers had the alternative of travelling on coastal liners. Travel by sea had been an attractive alternative to the stagecoach, but while the stagecoach disappeared, driven into extinction by the railways, superior in speed and low in cost of travel, the coasting ships adopted steam, which cut the passage from London to Edinburgh from three or four days to thirty hours.

The variety of services and routes offered by the shipping companies seems incredible to us today, with services from London to many East Coast destinations and round the coast to Bristol, Liverpool and Glasgow. Obviously, the Irish Sea services were busier and more varied than those along the South Coast or the East Coast, but to give an idea of how indirect some services could be, there were sailings by the Antrim Iron Ore Company to Teesside, round the north of Scotland. Many such ships accommodated just small numbers of passengers, but others could carry as many as 300, or even more when a substantial number of deck passengers could be carried. One attraction was, of course, the number of direct services, especially if the journey was to be partly by ship anyway, as to Ireland, the Scottish islands or Channel Islands, but another attraction was cost. The shipping companies offered much lower fares than the railways.

Sir Richard Moon would have had such low-cost competition in mind, just as his successors today would have the speed of air travel.

The winter schedule for 1887–88 to Glasgow was eased by five minutes, but that to Edinburgh reverted to the previous ten-hour schedule because the Caledonian Railway held the Edinburgh portion at Carlisle for a full twenty-five minutes, which passengers must have found frustrating.

A further round was fired by the East Coast companies in November 1887 when they announced in Bradshaw, the monthly railway time-table book, which covered all of the British Isles (all of Ireland being part of the UK at the time), that the 'Special Scotch Express' would at last carry '3rd class passengers from London ... to Edinbro [sic]'. Connections from stations serving the south of England and from Broad Street were also announced, but curiously, despite calls en route, third-class passengers were not to be carried to anywhere south of Edinburgh, equally curiously abbreviated as 'Edinbro', upsetting many Scots.

Despite such insensitivity towards the Scots language, this concession meant that the East Coast route held the speed advantage over its rivals and was now able to attract the third-class passenger as well.

While the pre-grouping railway is often presented as being fragmented and uncoordinated, this was only half true. It was fragmented, albeit in a different way than today, as more than a hundred companies were at least vertically integrated and owned their own track and rolling stock, while many of the minor companies conceded the provision of services, and especially passenger services, to their larger neighbours. It was certainly far from uncoordinated, thanks to the efforts of the Railway Clearing House, which did far more than simply balance receipts and expenditure between the companies. It also pressed for standardization of such matters as signalling and head-codes to facilitate through running. Through services between London and Scotland would not have been possible without close collaboration between railway companies, and by this time such joint ventures had extended beyond the through East and West Coast routes to other services, including those between South Wales and the north-west of England. The most extreme example was eventually to be the provision of through carriages, and in summer through trains, including, as mentioned earlier, that between Aberdeen and Penzance. There

LONDON AND NORTH WESTERN AND CALEDONIAN RAILWAYS.

WEST COAST ROUTE TO and FROM

SCOTLAND.

Shortest Route to and from GLASGOW.

CORRIDOR, LUNCHEON, DINING, AND SLEEPING CARS.

COMMENCING JULY 10th, 1922. Week Days. | **Sun. ngt & Mon. mrn.**

STATIONS.	h mrn	mrn	mrn	g aft	aft	aft	a mrn	a aft	b aft	b aft	aft	mrn	b aft	d aft	b aft	a aft	aft	aft	aft
London (Euston) ......dep		5 0	6 45	10 0		1 30		7 30	9 20		11 0	11 0	1140	11 45	7 40	9 30	11 0	1140
Birmingham (New St.) ,,	3 j 0	7 15	9 10	11 0	12 15	2 50	8 20		10 50			12 25	6 50	10 15		
Liverpool { Lime Street ,,			h					1040		12 45	12 45	1245	9 V 0	12 45		
{ Exchange.. ,,	9 47	9 47	12 40		3 20	5 8		1250	1 50		1 40	1 50		
Manchester { Exchange ,,						5 0	1055		1 10	1 10	1 10		1115	1 10		
{ Victoria. ,,	9 40	9 40	12 30		3 0		mrn	mrn				mrn	2 55		mrn	mrn
Carlisle..............arr.	1245	1 19	3 25	3 58	4 9	6 25	7 44	8 27	1 40	2 14	4 0	5 0	5 16	5 33	6 40	6 20	2 14	4 46	5 16	6 40
Edinburgh (Princes St.) arr.	3 20	4 5	6 0		6 30	9X18	10 10	11 0			8 0	8 15		9 0		8 0	
Glasgow (Central)..... ,,	3 20	4 22	6	5 6 30		9X15	10 10	11 0		6 55	7 40		8 09	35	9 0		7 16	9 35
Greenock (Central)..... ,,	4 58	5 23	7 25	7 25		10 37	11Y31			7 55	8V48		9 15	1030		8 48	1030
Gourock .... ,,	4 52	5 41	7 39	7 39		10 51	11Y45			8 10	9 H 0		9 29	1012		9 0	1042
Oban.................. ,,		9 55				4 44	4 44	9 55	9 55		2 50		9 55		2 50
Perth................. ,,		5 37		8 10		12 35	1235	5 55	35		9 12	9 37		5 35		9 12
Dundee (West)......... ,,		7 22		8 58				6 50	6 50		10 5	1022		6 50		10 5
Dunkeld............... ,,		8 6				2F42	F4	6 21	6 21		10 6		6 21		10 6
Inverness via Dunk'ld ,,						6F0	6F0	9 25	1015		4 42		9 40		4 42
ABERDEEN............. ,,		9 5		10 35		3 03	0	7 40	7 40		11 50	1155		7 40		11 50
Ballater.............. ,,								9 45	9 45		5 0		9 45		5 0
Inverness via Aberd'n ,,						8F50	8F50	1155	1155		6 21		1155		6 21

Week Days. | Sun. from Scotland.

	mrn	mrn	mrn	mrn	mrn	aft	aft	mrn	aft	aft	aft	b	d	aft	aft	mrn	aft	aft
Inverness via Aberd'n dep.								7 40		b	b		1250	1250	b	d	
Ballater................ ,,				6 30	6 50			9 55			3 35	3 35			1 10
ABERDEEN........... ,,				6 30		9 30		12 30	aft		7 30	7 45			1 10
Inverness via Dunk'ld ,,	h	b	h	1120	aft	8 10	a	a	10 30	mrn	4 30		4 30	a
Dunkeld................ ,,				7 51	mrn	10 6			1 10	aft				3 0
Dundee (West)......... ,,				8 0	mrn	1110			2 25	7 5	9 09	15		3 0
Perth.................. ,,				9	mrn	1150			3 25	9 10	9 45	10 0		3 50
Oban.................. ,,				5 40	mrn	8 45			11 45 mrn	5 30		5 30		
Gourock .... ,,		8 20	8 20				1145	2 50	3 50	aft	8 0	9 5	9 59	59	5	3 15
Greenock (Central).... ,,		8 32	8 32				1155	2 59	4 1		8 11	9 15	9 159	159	15	3 24
Glasgow (Central)..... ,,		10 0	1010				1 30	4 10	5 30		9 30	1030	1110	1110	1116	10 0	5 30	1030
Edinburgh (Princes St.) ,,				1010		1 30		4 10	5 30	9 20		1030	mrn	10 0	5 40	1030
Carlisle.............. arr.	12 0	12	1412	1252	1252	3 38	3 48	6 50	8 23	12 5	1 10	1 0	1 25	1 56	1 50	2 8	1235	8 20	1 0
Manchester { Exchange arr.	aft		aft	,,		aft	aft	aft			7 27	1056	mrn	mrn	mrn	mrn	mrn	mrn
{ Victoria.. ,,	3 35		3 50	4 35		7 2	1035	12 18				5 50	6 5		4 15
Liverpool { Lime St... ,,								12 45						12 25
{ Exchange.. ,,	3 25		3 45	4 43	7	5 57	51025					6 06	15	4 22
Birmingham (New St.) ,,	5 17		6 40		9 45	2 15				6 327	11	7 23	2 15	6 13
London (Euston)....... ,,	6 30		7 30	1030	5 0	6 55	7 407	308	08 20	7 30	5 0	7 30

SLEEPING SALOONS ON NIGHT TRAINS.

a CORRIDOR, DINING, AND REFRESHMENT CAR EXPRESS.   **b** Not on Saturday nights.   **d** Saturday night and Sunday morning.   **F** No connecting Trains to these Stations on Sunday mornings.   **g** Corridor, Luncheon, and Tea Car Express.   **h** Luncheon Car Express.   **j** Leaves Birmingham 3 10 mrn. on Mondays.   **q** On Saturdays arrives Greenock 5 31 aft. and Gourock 5 45 aft.   **R** On Sundays arrives Greenock 9 15 and Gourock 9 29 mrn.   **s** Saturdays only.   **T** Calls at Dunkeld when required to pick up passengers. Notice to be given at the Station.   **V** Via Newton-le-Willows.   **X** On Saturdays arrives Edinburgh 9 23 aft., and Glasgow 9 20 aft.   **Y** On Wednesdays and Saturdays arrives Greenock 11 42 aft. and Gourock 11 56 aft.   **Z** Sunday mornings excepted.

ARTHUR WATSON, General Manager, L. & N. W. Railway.
DONALD A. MATHESON, General Manager, Caledonian Railway.

July, 1922.

The pre-1922 railway was fragmented, but collaboration between companies ensured through services, facilitated by the Railway Clearing House. This advertisement from a 1922 edition of *Bradshaw's Railway Guide* shows that the West Coast was the shortest to and from Glasgow, but could not be the quickest as by this time both routes had coordinated their through running times.

EASTERN GROUP OF RAILWAYS.

EAST COAST ROUTE.

ENGLAND & SCOTLAND

Via Forth and Tay Bridges.

FOR TRAIN SERVICE, SEE PAGES 332, 728, 734, 776, and 782:

THE ONLY ACTUAL "COAST" ROUTE.

Quickest Route

LONDON & EDINBURGH

(KING'S CROSS)   (WAVERLEY)

IN 8½ HOURS.

RESTAURANT CARS attached to Day Trains,
SLEEPING CARS attached to Night Trains

between

LONDON (King's Cross) and... {
EDINBURGH,
GLASGOW,
FORT WILLIAM,
DUNDEE,
ABERDEEN,
PERTH,
INVERNESS.

The pre-1922 East Coast route was more complicated as three railway companies were involved, and the North British was not allowed to handle trains unless they ran north of Edinburgh. It was not the 'coast route' as passengers only saw the coast north of Newcastle.

The sad remains of the original Tay Bridge, with the gap where the bridge had collapsed. The bases of the piers for the original bridge are still easy to spot today.

The sole survivor of the ill-fated train was the locomotive, seen here after being salvaged. Given the height from which it fell, it is surprising that the damage was not worse.

Cantilever bridges were a novel and untried concept, so this experiment with three men was arranged to show the sceptics how it would work. Designed at a time when trains rarely exceeded 400 tons, until recently it handled coal trains of up to 1,700 tons gross weight.

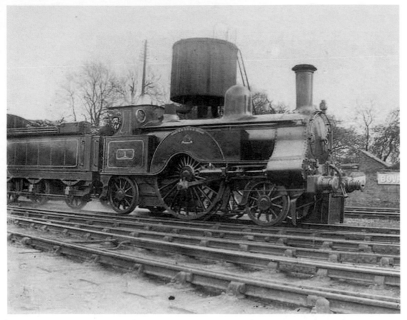

At the start of the 1888 races, observers were surprised when the LNWR opted for an older locomotive, the twenty-five-year-old 2–2–2 *Waverley*, to take the first racing train out of Euston. This is the *Lady of the Lake*, the class leader and so identical to *Waverley*.

By contrast, the Great Northern used its Stirling 4–2–2 eight-foot singles such as No. 776, shown here beside a turntable. Eventually, increasing locomotive weight and power meant that coupled wheels were necessary, but at the time, the single driving wheel still had much to offer.

(HMRS/Hilton ABA 813)

Another Stirling 4–2–2 eight-foot single, in steam and with a train of six-wheel coaches, although only the end of the leading carriage can be seen. This was a typical railway scene at the time, although the location is unknown.

All of the races were northbound, but the 1895 races often had the LNWR allocate the Teutonic-class No. 1307 *Coptic*, seen here after arrival at Euston, to the racing trains. (*HMRS/Tatchell ADE 121*)

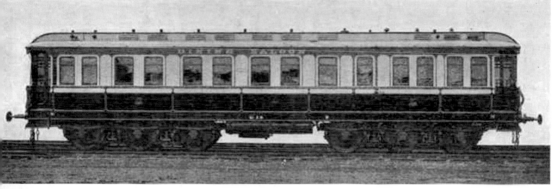

The races occurred at the time when not only were single-wheel locomotives being challenged by compound locomotives, usually with double driving wheels, but six-wheel carriages were giving way to bogie carriages, such as this LNWR example. Both types appeared on the racing trains of 1895.

This is Caledonian Railway Lambie 4–4–0 No. 70, at an unidentified location. Note the later style of GNR-type cut-away driving cab. The Lambie 4–4–0s were developed from the Drummond locomotives with the same wheel notation, but the Lambie locomotives had higher boiler pressure. Both types were used in the races. (*HMRS/Tatchell ADC 124*)

A southbound express leaves the Forth Bridge, around 1900, headed by a North British M1-class, later redesignated 'M', 4–4–0. The bridge saved time and money by avoiding the need for train ferries, but trains were from the start limited to 40mph while crossing. (*HMRS/Tatchell ADE 626*)

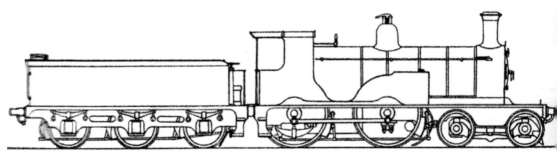

An outline of a Drummond 4–4–0.

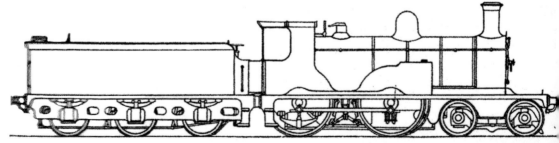

An outline of a Lambie 4–4–0, with the original style of driving cab. The different position of the safety valve is the most obvious difference.

A contemporary impression of a Great Northern mail train in 1894 – the nets for receiving mail as stations were passed without stopping can be seen on the leading carriage.

The 'latest type of North-Eastern engine' in 1894. The NER provided some exciting rides for the observers as they charged towards Edinburgh Waverley. This was an M1-class.

By contrast, this was the latest express locomotive of the same year on the Great Northern, still with single large driving wheels. Although the locomotive shown had 7ft 6in wheels, others had 8ft. The image is credited to J.R.Thompson of Doncaster, presumably hired by the GNR works.

By contrast to the earlier image, this is a contemporary image of an LNWR express, also in 1894. Note that the carriages appear to be six-wheelers, which would have given an uncomfortable ride at speed.

The famous LNWR Precedent-class No. 790 *Hardwicke*, with which Driver B. 'Big Ben' Robinson and Fireman W. Wolstencroft, on the night of 15/16 July 1895, took the night express from Crewe to Carlisle. The same locomotive handled this working for the next nine nights.

A shot of an express being drawn by a GNR Stirling single-wheeler. This was typical of the trains of the day. Note the six-wheel carriages behind the locomotive, although bogie carriages seem to be present further back.

were also joint lines, such as the Somerset & Dorset and the Midland & Great Northern Joint Railway.

It soon became clear to the senior officers of the Great Northern that their counterparts at the London & North Western were not going to be content with the East Coast route's growing domination of the traffic between London and Edinburgh.

At first, it was simply a question of playing catch-up. Giving as little notice as possible, the LNWR announced that from 2 June 1888, the 'Day Scotch Express' would have a whole hour cut from its timings to both Glasgow and Edinburgh. The East Coast was no longer the quickest route between the two capitals. This was a significant step forward and an equally significant change in policy at Euston, with the average speeds north of Willesden Junction exceeding 50mph all the way to Carlisle. The best was between Rugby and Crewe, at 51.5mph. The big gain for Edinburgh passengers was that the Caledonian cut the time the train was left waiting at Carlisle to a more business-like seven minutes, with the portions not separated until the train arrived at Carstairs.

In accelerating the West Coast service, both the LNWR and the Caledonian used double-heading of locomotives whenever the train load required it. By contrast, the Great Northern's chief mechanical engineer, Patrick Stirling, positively forbade double-heading and ensured that this was not possible by not having brake connections on the front buffer beams of his express locomotives. This policy was already hampering operations, as the East Coast route had enjoyed a tremendous surge in third-class passengers as a result of admitting them to the 10.00am departures.

In mid-June, the East Coast companies finally responded by announcing that from 1 July, the 10.00am 'Special Scotch Express' would reach Edinburgh half an hour earlier, at 8.30pm. The Great Northern and the North Eastern both cut ten minutes from their schedules, but the rest was a cut of ten minutes in the luncheon stop at York. As with the West Coast, the new schedule produced running in excess of 50mph, but even so, the best averages were not much higher at 51mph between King's Cross and Grantham, and 51.6mph between Grantham and York. North of York, the average speed to Newcastle was 49.8mph and then 49.5mph on to Berwick-on-Tweed, with 44.7mph onwards to Edinburgh Waverley.

The ability of the East Coast companies to respond so quickly to the West Coast challenge caught Euston by surprise. The West Coast companies had spent the winter preparing their new timetable; the East Coast companies had spent weeks. This was a blow to the company that had the main Royal Mail route between London and Scotland, and which proudly conveyed Her Majesty Queen Victoria on her annual autumn visit to Balmoral.

Senior officers at Euston wanted a further acceleration so that the West Coast could become the fastest route once again, and in this they were supported by pressure from the Caledonian. The peak period for summer traffic was upon the Anglo-Scottish railway companies and much business was at stake. Sir Richard Moon was the obstacle to progress, so the London & North Western set up a special committee, drawn from its directors, to review the situation. Not surprisingly, the announcement soon came that from 1 August, the service between London and Edinburgh would take eight and a half hours. Effectively, the LNWR's directors were overruling their own chairman!

The new schedule saw the luncheon stop at Preston again cut to twenty minutes for the Edinburgh passengers, but the LNWR did not make any acceleration in its schedule between London and Preston, doubtless feeling that they had done enough and the next round of reduced journey times should come from the Caledonian. The reason why the Edinburgh passengers were chosen for a hasty lunch was that in the new timetable the Edinburgh and Glasgow portions divided at Preston, and it was sensible to make good use of the luncheon interval to marshal the two portions. The Edinburgh portion resumed its journey at 2.42pm, while the Glasgow portion followed at the June timetable time of 2.47pm, giving the passengers an extra five minutes for their lunch.

The parsimonious LNWR may have surprised many by adding an extra ninety train miles to its 'Day Scotch Express', but the heavy train had often needed to be double-headed over Shap, so the extra cost may have been very little and it could have been that locomotive miles were unchanged, certainly at peak periods. The Edinburgh train was now accorded priority and when it reached Carlisle at 4.27pm, there was no hanging around. The LNWR locomotive was quickly uncoupled and steamed out of the way so that the Caledonian locomotive could take over and the train was away at 4.32pm, no fewer than fifteen minutes before the Glasgow train departed, and off non-stop to Edinburgh.

The Caledonian also raised its speed, to 50.8mph, in line with the speeds being attained by the LNWR south of the border. To some extent, there was a degree of cheating in that the train was rarely more than 100 tons, so that even Beattock Summit presented little challenge.

Clearly, the LNWR expected the East Coast companies to respond to the challenge of the new timetable. The prompt response to the June acceleration had shaken the LNWR's management, and they were determined that they would not make any further announcements until the last minute. The Great Northern was certain that something was afoot, and while they did not resort to industrial espionage, the superintendent of the line sent members of his staff along the road to Euston to study timetables, and eavesdrop on conversations on the platforms and in the buffets.

The Media Takes an Interest

Railways were not the source of interest at the time that they later became. There were few railway enthusiasts, and trainspotters were virtually unknown. The announcements by the East and West Coast companies had attracted little attention in the press, and it was not until three regular correspondents started writing letters to editors that the newspapers began to wake up to what was happening.

One of these individuals was W.M. Acworth, who was a regular correspondent to *The Times*, and had taken care to become known to the senior management of the LNWR at Euston. Another was Norman D. Macdonald, a Scottish advocate (barrister), who had friends amongst the senior management of both the Caledonian and North British Railways, while the third was an Anglo-Catholic priest, the Rev. W.J. Scott, who knew both F.P. Cockshott, the GNR's Superintendent of the Line, and his assistant, J. Alexander, at King's Cross. These three men had independently had their interest roused by the LNWR's announcement that the 10.00am departure from Euston would reach Edinburgh in eight and a half hours.

Alerted to the competition between the country's two longest trunk routes, in August, a quiet month for news (hence the term 'silly season'), reporters were sent to keep an eye on developments. No reporter wants to admit to his editor that he hasn't a story, and so even in the quality newspapers, any developments were bound to be given a dramatic edge.

Railway management teams today would be delighted with the publicity and the enthusiasm, but at the time railway safety was nowhere near as good as it is today. Accidents were fairly common, and while the mass of the population had become accustomed to the higher speed of rail travel, there were still those afraid of speed, including Queen Victoria, whose aversion to fast running was made known after her first railway journey. Her fears were not groundless, as the LNWR, for all its strengths, did not have the best reputation for safety and continuous braking was not available on all of its trains at the time. The news coverage led to the editors of the letters pages being inundated with correspondence warning of the dangers of excessive speed. Nevertheless, many of the worst railway accidents, such as the Tay Bridge, which collapsed, and Armagh, which was caused by a runaway rake of carriages left behind after the locomotive could not pull the entire train up an incline, had not been caused by speeding.

Those who were of a nervous disposition sometimes used the comfort and safety of the footplatemen as an excuse, but they were given short shrift by the magazine *The Engineer*, in its August 1888 issue.

> The sympathy extended by a section of the public to the drivers and firemen is about as well placed as it would be if it were expended on the jockeys who ride the Derby. To drive one of the flying expresses is the highest pinnacle of honour to which a driver can attain, and not the least enjoyable moment of a man's life is that when he draws up to the platform with three minutes' time to spare, and finds himself and his engine the centre of attraction for an admiring crowd.

The press were not to be disappointed. On the first day of the West Coast companies' new timetable, Wednesday 1 August, the East Coast train ran from King's Cross to Edinburgh Waverley in just eight hours! The combined efforts of the Great Northern and North Eastern (as the North British was not allowed to handle trains between Newcastle and Edinburgh) had ruined the party for the LNWR and the Caledonian.

The Railway News carried an account the following Saturday, 4 August.

> We have been favoured by Mr Cockshott, superintendent of the Great Northern Railway, with the official copy of the guards' journals of the running of the two portions of the new ten o'clock Scotch express at the accelerated speed adopted on the East Coast route on the 1st inst. We are also informed that on each day of the new service the trains have arrived at their destination before the advertised times, and that all trains have been fairly filled,

the majority of the carriages having their full complement. The train was made up of two saloons, two third-class vehicles, three composites, and two brake-vans, in all nine vehicles, exclusive of engine and tender. The run was made with four stops only –viz, Grantham 105, York 188, Newcastle 272, Berwick 312, Edinburgh 392 miles. The time occupied on the journey was eight hours less seven minutes ... The average speed, including stoppages, was a small fraction over 49 miles per hour; excluding stoppages, the average running speed, including 'slowing' and 'starting', was 53½ miles per hour. The highest speed in the record was the Retford section, the running being 19 miles in 19 minutes. The run from Hitchin to Peterborough, of 44 miles, was made in 45 minutes. The second portion of the train, leaving King's Cross at 10.05 – five minutes after the first – was timed to arrive at Edinburgh at 6.30, but arrived at 6.25, making the run in 8 hours and 20 minutes – a reasonable and prudent distance between the two trains being necessary.

All this came as the railways were preparing for the busiest period of the year, with the August bank holiday, at that time held on the first Monday of August, approaching, and the railways having the highly profitable traffic for the start of the shooting season on 12 August in prospect.

The LNWR lost no time in convening a meeting of the Directors' Special Committee for the following day. By the afternoon, the LNWR and the CR were able to announce that from Monday, 6 August, they would run from Euston to Edinburgh Princes Street in just eight hours. George Whale, the LNWR's Locomotive Running Superintendent, was despatched to Glasgow that very night, accompanied by George Neele, the Superintendent of the Line, to meet their Caledonian counterparts at Buchanan Street. The meeting must have been very business-like for, having arrived at Buchanan Street at 7.00am, they left again at 10.00am on that morning's 'Special Scotch Express' for Euston, having agreed that the Caledonian would cut the running time between Carlisle and Edinburgh from 118 minutes to 112 minutes for the 100.6 miles.

On the return journey, the two men saw the district officers and the locomotive and traffic superintendents of the company at Carlisle, Preston, Crewe and Rugby, all summoned by telegram so that they could be told what was expected of them on the following Monday.

Most significant of the changes was that the train was to run in two portions from Euston, while the Edinburgh portion was to leave first and run non-stop to Crewe. At the time, this was the longest non-stop run in the British Isles. It was an achievement that the East Coast companies could not emulate at the time, because it depended on the locomotive picking up water from the water troughs that the LNWR had, but neither the GNR nor NER had yet installed. The schedule called for the train to run to Crewe at an average speed of 52.7mph, then on to Preston at 52.8mph, and, after a twenty-minute stop for luncheon, the journey to Carlisle would be accomplished at an average speed of 54mph. For its part, the Caledonian would put in a similar performance with an average speed between Carlisle and Edinburgh of 53.8mph.

Many have commented on the fact that the arduous stretches between Preston and Carlisle and between Carlisle and Edinburgh were faster than the fairly level running south of Preston, but the southern end of the LNWR was the company's busiest, and finding suitable paths for not one but two express trains on a busy bank holiday Monday was a challenge.

When the new schedule was announced, the senior officers of the company were besieged by reporters, as were the footplatemen on the day, as the 10.00am departure became an attraction. Euston was crowded with spectators for this new sport. Many bets were placed before the departure.

Anti-climax

As the crowds waited expectantly, there was a sense of anti-climax when the locomotive arrived, backing down to the train. Those who knew the steam locomotives of the day were expecting one of Webb's compound locomotives, renowned for their power and good running, or at the very least a 'Precedent'. Instead of the latest in motive power, they were shocked to see a 2–2–2 Lady of the Lake-class, some twenty-five years old. Surely there had been a mistake, or perhaps the booked locomotive had failed? Neither had happened, and it was soon clear that locomotive No. 806 was a deliberate choice, for her name was *Waverley*, really throwing down the gauntlet to the East Coast companies. Not only that, but the weekend must have been spent bestowing much tender loving care on the locomotive, for her black paint shone and her nameplate glistened. The LNWR was not known for being kind to its locomotives, but *Waverley* stood out amidst the smoky confines of the old Euston station.

Many doubted whether she could do all that was expected of her. She would have been dwarfed had she been beside the Stirling 'eight-footer' that at that moment would have been coupled to the East Coast 10.00am departure from King's Cross. Yet *Waverley* was expected to make the longest non-stop run attempted anywhere, despite her age and small size. On the other hand, the train consisted of just four carriages and, at the time, that meant a load of no more than eighty tons.

Of course, most of the onlookers knew little about railways and, as the whistle blew and she departed right on time at 10.00am, there were loud cheers from those on the platform, while others had swarmed on to the arrival platform, Platform 1, and on to the road bridge that overlooked the station approaches.

The doubters were soon reassured as signal boxes telegraphed news of her progress. Rugby, 82.6 miles from Euston, was passed in ninety-four minutes, and then Stafford, at 133.6 miles, in 148½ minutes, giving an average of 54mph. The driver had to ease back so that she did not arrive ahead of time at Crewe, where engines were changed and a 'Precedent', *Vulcan*, took over. At this point, the timetable limited what could be achieved, as there had to be the scheduled luncheon interval at Preston. How the LNWR must have wished for dining cars or even Pullman cars at this stage – but these were much heavier than the relatively simple rolling stock then in widespread use. As it was, with just four carriages, *Vulcan* soared over Shap and then swept down into Carlisle.

At Carlisle, the Caledonian certainly played its part, for there waiting for the Edinburgh train was the company's latest locomotive, the first and at that time still the only 4–2–2, No. 123, chosen in preference to one of the company's 4–4–0s that were already known for their fine turn of speed. There could be no question of an early departure, as the timetable had to be observed, and that decreed that Carlisle should be left at 4.08pm, no earlier. Yet the choice of loco-motive proved to be inspired, as No. 123 raced over the 100.6 miles from Carlisle to Edinburgh in just 104 minutes instead of the 112 minutes scheduled, arriving at Princes Street eight minutes early at 5.52pm.

This achievement was not a one-off, as for the rest of the month the same locomotive covered the distance between Carlisle and

Edinburgh in an average time of 107¾ minutes, giving an average speed of 56mph despite the climb up Beattock.

The eastern companies clearly had not anticipated such a swift and decisive response, given the previous relatively lengthy period between the western companies announcing a new timetable and its implementation. This time, it had taken less than a week for the LNWR and the CR to match the GNR and NER's timings, and indeed unofficially better them. For a week both 10.00am departures took an official eight hours.

Norman Macdonald would wait daily for the East Coast train to steam into Waverley before leaping into a hansom cab and having the driver race along Princes Street to the station of that name, behind the Caledonian Hotel, to see if the West Coast train had arrived.

By this time, the story was international. On the evening of 6 August, a report of the inaugural eight-hour run was sent to the *New York Herald*, including the early arrival.

Perhaps the most interesting account was that by one of the passengers, a professional railwayman, no less a person than Sir Edward Watkin, the chairman of the Manchester Sheffield & Lincoln Railway, later to become the Great Central Railway when it finally reached London in 1899, the last company to do so, building a new terminus at Marylebone. Watkin, who had worked in Canada, recalled:

> I have travelled all over the world and I have never had a pleasanter journey. There was steadiness, noiselessness, continuity of speed; no rushing up and down, no block, except just once at Atherstone; always before time. It was capital in every way. And then the refreshment part – the lunch at Preston – soup, choice of meat, sweets, cheese, and a cup of coffee, and all for three shillings ... It is a *train de luxe*. The highest speed travelled was not more than 65mph. The great secret in getting a steady train is to have the vehicles the same length, the same weight, and all coupled well together. That was the case today, and I never experienced easier running.

One finds this just a little unrealistic – rose-tinted glasses come to mind. For a start, just twenty minutes to consume a meal of three or four courses, plus coffee, demands an ability to swallow food in tremendous haste. The LNWR had some of the best track, but was it that quiet and comfortable over jointed track? The block at Atherstone was due to a level crossing on what is now the A5, but at the time simply known as the Holyhead Road. This was a *cause célèbre* between the LNWR and the local authority, which at one time obtained an injunction against the company which, until it was lifted, forced all trains to slow to just 4mph at the crossing.

The Race Continues
That Friday, 10 August, the East Coast companies responded by announcing that from 13 August, the following Monday, the 10.00am from King's Cross was to travel to Edinburgh in just seven and three quarter hours. This was to be performed throughout the rest of August with a heavier train than that from Euston, with seven six-wheeled carriages, giving a total unladen weight of 100.5 tons. The schedule between King's Cross and Newcastle was unchanged, but the five-minute call at Berwick-on-Tweed was omitted, so that the run between Newcastle and Edinburgh was run non-stop in just 137 minutes for the 124.4 miles.

Unlike the LNWR, the GNR used its most modern locomotives, with no fewer than ten different ones being used during what remained of August. The classes included both the 8-foot bogie singles and Patrick Stirling's new 7½-foot 2–2–2 locomotives. There was reasonable consistency in performance, so that for the rest of the month the average run over the 105.5 miles between King's Cross and Grantham was at 55.7mph, while the slowest trip was at 54.5mph and the fastest, by No. 233, took 105 minutes to reach Grantham, an average speed of just over 60mph. Just as the LNWR was hampered by the need to call at Preston for luncheon, so the GNR was restricted by the similar need to call at York. Between Grantham and York, just four different locomotives were used over the month.

The North Eastern Railway had not, hitherto, been known for high-speed running, and while not as severe as Shap or Beattock, there were nevertheless a number of fairly steep gradients on the line between Newcastle and Edinburgh. The locomotives used by the NER were the new 4–4–0 compounds which alternated with Tennant's 2–4–0s. The 80.6 miles between York and Newcastle was scheduled to take ninety-three minutes, but sometimes the luncheon interval at York was exceeded, and the average running time was just eighty-three and a half minutes, giving an average speed of 58mph. Even better was to occur north of Newcastle, especially when Driver R. Nicholson was in the cab, on one occasion reaching an average of 59.3mph between Newcastle and Edinburgh. By comparison, before the races started, the average between Newcastle and Berwick-on-Tweed was 49.5mph and that onwards to Edinburgh was 44.9mph.

Up until this time, the timetable was king. After all, no railway company wanted to lose revenue by leaving passengers behind. All this changed on 13 August. To try to steal the East Coast companies' thunder, the West Coast companies simply told their drivers to run trains as far ahead of the schedule as they could manage. Trains left the terminus on time, but en route they left intermediate stations as soon as they were ready, even if that meant an early departure.

Nevertheless, working at the extremes of performance meant that the condition of the locomotive, as well as the skills and stamina of the driver and fireman, resulted in varying degrees of success.

The little Ramsbottom 2–2–2 *Waverley* once again showed that she was up to the challenge, running from Euston to Crewe in 166 minutes at an average speed of 57mph, indicating much running at 60mph and above, as the start from Euston would have been followed by a steep uphill climb through a tunnel. This enabled the Precedent-class that took over at Crewe to leave fourteen minutes early, taking fifty-six minutes for the run to Preston, against a later best of fifty minutes, while the ninety-nine minutes onwards to Carlisle compared unfavourably with a best performance of ninety minutes, so that the arrival at Carlisle was just sixteen minutes early. The day was saved by the Caledonian's No. 123, which got the train to Princes Street at 5.38pm, twenty-two minutes ahead of schedule.

This sparkling performance was all the better for the fact that on that day the East Coast companies suffered one of the few late arrivals of the races. As a result, the following day, 14 August, the NER double-headed the train from York onwards, so that it arrived at Waverley at 5.32pm, thirteen minutes early.

End of the Races
Despite the desire to be fastest, 14 August effectively marked the end of the races. That day a conference was held in London between the East and West Coast companies. The companies agreed that the East Coast should be allowed to continue at a through journey time of seven and three quarter hours, while the West Coast would take eight hours between London and Edinburgh. One of those involved, George

Neele, Superintendent of the Line at the LNWR, explained in his memoirs:

> The advent of the holidays had a very tranquillising effect on the racing spirit, the affair was at an end, and in September our timetable reverted to the table in force for July, showing 6.30pm as the time for the London & North Western express to be due in Edinburgh, the East Coast showing 6.15pm as their arrival ... till a further disturbance arose in 1895.

One might wonder just what had been achieved, as there was clearly no lasting benefit to the passenger. Autumn saw a half hour added to the best of the summer schedules. The winter schedules, however, did show much improvement over those of a year earlier.

This was a time when the railways were facing public and parliamentary criticism, and legislation that affected their income. On 18 August, *The Railway News* saw fit to comment on the races and the outcome.

> Whatever the shareholders may think of the matter, the public, at all events, have reason to be grateful for the efforts which are being made for the protection of their interests, and the increased facilities which are being afforded them by our railways. Coincident with the passing of the Railway and Canal Rates Bill, which Sir Richard Moon declares will be so injurious to the railway companies, the directors of the North-Western commenced an accelerated train service to Scotland as a further boon and concession to the public. The 'boon' should be the more gratefully accepted as it was wholly unsolicited and gratuitous on the part of the company. It was heaping coals of fire on the heads of the exacting and ever-complaining public. Parliament, he said, acting in the united capacity of plaintiff, judge, and jury, had ruthlessly struck out of the bill the provisions which gave the companies an equivalent for the loss they would sustain by the new classification of the tolls. The 'greedy' public had got all that they had asked ... However the railway companies are not vindictive, and to show that they bore no malice, presented the 'greedy' public with an accelerated train service to Scotland, to commence on August 6 – the day by which it was anticipated the oppressive traders' bill would become law ... Meanwhile it is as

well to bear in mind that this 'war of speed' has not been caused by any action or decree of the Board of Trade, whose interference in railway matters is so much deprecated at Euston and elsewhere. The public, of course, display their accustomed interest in these racing exploits, and in time we may expect to see as much excitement shown in railway racing as in former times was displayed on the Mississippi boats.

Nevertheless, all was not over. On 31 August, those boarding that day's 10.00am departure from King's Cross for Edinburgh got wind of a further attempt. The news spread that the 'Special Scotch Express' would be despatched from intermediate stations as soon as the train was ready. The express was indeed seven minutes early at Grantham, but onwards to York progress was marred by a short signal check just south of Doncaster, and then at Selby the swing bridge operator accorded priority to a barge full of hay, so only an additional thirty seconds was gained as the train arrived at York seven and a half minutes early at 1.22½pm. Despite this, the luncheon interval was extended, possibly, one wonders, because the caterers were not ready for the early arrival of the hungry horde of travellers off the train. Worse, while the passengers were back aboard and ready for the journey to resume at 1.42, the locomotive was nowhere to be seen. At 1.45pm a Tennant 2–4–0, No. 1475, appeared and backed onto the train, but coupling was slow and it was not until 1.49 that the train was ready to go, just a minute earlier than shown in the timetable.

Although it seemed that the NER was determined to stick to the published timetable, the passengers were in for a surprise. Despite a check at Ferryhill for one and three quarter minutes, and further checks approaching Chester-le-Street, the 80.5 miles from York to Newcastle were covered in 83¼ minutes, so the train arrived ten minutes early and this time also left ten minutes early. Once again, Driver R. Nicholson took over at Newcastle, this time with the new compound 4–4–0 No. 117, and he pressed the locomotive to complete the 124.4 miles to Edinburgh in 130 minutes, so that arrival at Waverley was at 5.27pm, eighteen minutes early.

This gave the East Coast companies the final word on the races with the fastest timing of all, giving an average speed, start to stop, between London and Edinburgh of 52.7mph including station calls and the extended luncheon interval. The West Coast companies had achieved their best on 13 August, of 52.3mph, although as mentioned earlier the locomotive had not been steamed well between Crewe and Carlisle and far better might have been achieved.

In fact, that winter the early summer timings were maintained, so that the East Coast schedule during 1888/89 was forty-five minutes faster than during the previous winter, and on London to Edinburgh, that of the West Coast was no less than ninety minutes faster. So while the best timings were not retained, overall schedules had been much improved.

The Railway News summed up the gains in its edition of 1 September 1888.

> The 'Race to Edinburgh' will cease today (Saturday) when the extra expresses will be withdrawn by both companies, and the journey will in future be performed in eight hours and a-half, or at the rate of 47 miles per hour, lunch and all other stoppages included. But in return for this, two other accelerations are promised. The up train from Perth, now leaving at 8.45am, will leave at 8.30, form a connection with the 10 o'clock express from Glasgow, and arrive in London at 7 o'clock, a whole hour earlier than at present. The 10 o'clock up train from Edinburgh will run in the same time as the corresponding down train – will arrive, that is, at Euston at 6.30 instead of 7.00.

It would be wrong to see the tighter schedules as being the only benefit to the passenger at this time. During the racing month, the Midland Railway, the East Coast and the West Coast companies between them had no fewer than twenty-nine trains running between London and Scotland that could be counted as expresses, in that they had an average speed of more than 40mph including stops. In 1885, there had only been sixteen. There were also additional expresses between the cities of the north of England and Scotland, and a number of other trains that missed being counted as expresses because of the additional stops. These were apart from the shooting season specials.

In contrast to many European countries, these were not exclusive trains with costly supplements. Most were open to all classes of passenger. There was even an overnight express for horses and carriages so that these would be waiting for their owners when they arrived. One LNWR sleeper did not call at a station between Euston and Perth, so that the slumbers of its passengers would not be disturbed by passengers boarding or alighting, although stops had to be made to change locomotives.

The magazine *Engineering* summed up the position admirably.

The 2nd of June, the 1st of July, the 1st of August, and the 6th of August 1888 will long be remembered in the railway world as red-letter days. They mark the stages in a struggle for the Scotch traffic which is only just beginning, and which will grow fiercer as the Forth Bridge nears completion. For years the London & North Western Company has been calmly sleeping like the enchanted princess in the fairy tale, secure in its comfortable surroundings which defend it against the intrusion of strangers. But now the period of the magic is ending, not with the kiss of the enamoured prince, but with a challenge from another princess, which purposes seizing some of the territory held so easily.

Chapter 8

Racing Again

There was, inevitably, a sense of anti-climax once the races had finished, but at least there had been tangible gains in schedules. It was also an uneasy peace, for, as *Engineering* had pointed out, the forthcoming completion of the Forth Bridge would mark a further stage in the struggle for the Scottish traffic. Indeed, many of the ordinary newspapers and magazines had seen the races not as a contest in themselves, but as a series of 'trial heats' as a prelude to the 'real fight'. This contrasted with the reality, which was that the contestants had agreed minimum timings for the services linking London and Edinburgh.

Many believe that the Forth Bridge was too big a project for one company, but that is to overlook the point, which is that the construction of the Tay Bridge, the expenses associated with its collapse and the building of a replacement, had left the North British Railway so weakened that it needed the assistance of the North Eastern and Great Northern as well as the Midland Railway to be able to build this massive and elegant monument to the steam railway. The four companies shared the cost, but not equally, as the Midland accounted for thirty per cent. This was not generosity; it was because the Midland was by far the most enthusiastic, for it could see the prospect of expresses not only from London to the Highlands, with a successful business in traffic to and from the Midlands, but from Bristol and Gloucester as well.

The significance of the Forth Bridge was such that the King's Cross routes became the shortest to many important destinations north of the Forth. Perth became 440.9 miles from King's Cross against 449.9 from Euston, while Aberdeen was 523.2 miles from King's Cross, but 539.7 miles from Euston. These were substantial reductions in mileage, but the biggest cut was between London and Dundee, where the East Coast route was 451.9 miles against 471 on the West Coast, a very significant reduction of nineteen miles.

The bridges across the Forth and Tay, of course, were only one factor in the routes. These massive short-cuts across the wide firths were impressive in the mileage saved or the cut in delay in transferring onto a ferry or train ferry, but across Fife the North British had shown a lack of foresight for a railway that had planned two massive bridges, amongst the largest in the world at the time. The lines in Fife were little more than a collection of branch lines, rather than a section of a through express route. They were meant to serve the small communities and in particular the coalfields. There were tight curves and severe gradients, and junctions that were difficult to work efficiently. One of the most unwelcome obstacles along the line was the reverse curve in the middle of Kinghorn Tunnel.

In summary, over the 59¼ miles between Edinburgh and Dundee, in addition to the 40mph limit over the Forth Bridge, there were no fewer than six severe speed restrictions for junctions, many of them on the approach to steep gradients where a driver would like to have attained a brisk pace to help his locomotive surmount the summit. Such obstacles to good running included a bank at Inverkeithing of two miles at 1:94, which would have been fine if approached at 70mph, but which, following a permanent way slack to just 25mph, represented hard work. Even coasting down these steep banks had to be restricted to take the train safely through the slack at the foot.

While the line to Perth, swinging away northwards at Inverkeithing, had fewer speed restrictions, the gradients were more severe, including the eight-mile climb to Cowdenbeath and, continuing northwards, a steep six-mile descent from Glenfarg to Strathearn, with the fifteen miles between these two gradients sharply undulating and with many tight curves.

By contrast, while like many railways the Caledonian had been completed in sections, there was a controlling mind in Joseph Locke, the engineer, who saw it from the beginning as a through route from Glasgow to the Scottish north-east. Behind Locke was the Grand Junction Railway, which had held ambitions to equal those later held by the Midland. Bridges notwithstanding, north of Edinburgh the East Coast route was far weaker than the West Coast. The East Coast line between London and Edinburgh had been conceived and built in this forward-looking way, but either economy, the importance of local traffic or a failure to appreciate that the Forth and Tay would one day be bridged had left the North British route through Fife as the weakest link. It was also the case that the North British board had a well-deserved reputation for parsimony. Conversely, it seems fair to assume that, having met the cost of bridging the Tay and its contribution towards the cost of the bridge across the Forth, the North British lacked the funds to do what it should have done and build a new line across Fife, or at least a number of cut-offs to bypass the most difficult stretches. Of course, the extensive mining in the area could have made planning a route difficult and, for any substantial changes, Parliamentary approval would have had to be sought.

Looking at the railway map, many observers thought that any new rivalry once the Forth Bridge opened would be between London and Perth, but Aberdeen was the major prize. Not only was the city itself larger, not only did it have the then extensive fishing industry, but it was also the railhead for an area that grew considerable agricultural produce and, of course, carried out whisky distilling, as the city was within easy reach of Speyside. In short, provide a good service to Aberdeen and both Perth and Dundee would also benefit, especially the latter city, as a non-stop train between London, or even Edinburgh, and Aberdeen could not have been justified, and in any case, the time spent at these calls was as nothing compared to the time expended coping with the indifferent track, the gradients and the sharp curves.

Meanwhile, there was a change of command at the LNWR's headquarters at Euston. Sir Richard Moon retired in February 1891, while in March 1893 George Findlay, the general manager, died after several years of very poor health, during which he had to miss many important board meetings and lost the opportunity to influence the direction of the LNWR. Because of this, perhaps more significant even than Moon's successor was Findlay's replacement, Frederick Harrison, who happily proved to be a man of great energy. Under Harrison, the division of responsibilities between Findlay and the then secretary, Stephen Reay, ended. If this seems strange today, in most businesses at the time the secretary to the board exercised far wider general management functions than has become the case, and was not confined to recording the minutes of the meetings or providing advice and guidance on points of company law and procedure.

The Benefits of the Bridges *versus* the State of the Line
Until the Forth Bridge opened, the 10.00am departure from London King's Cross did not reach Aberdeen, known as the 'Granite City' or

the 'Silvery City'*, until 11.20pm, or more than thirteen hours after leaving London, while the overnight sleeper that left King's Cross at 8.00pm arrived in Aberdeen at 9.55am, taking an extra thirty-five minutes end-to-end compared with the day train. Once the bridge opened, the 10.00am reached Aberdeen at 10.20pm, saving a whole hour, while the 8.00pm arrived at 8.55am, again having saved an hour. Overnight trains to Perth left King's Cross at 7.45pm and 8.00pm, arriving at 5.50am and 6.15am respectively.

One problem with services to Aberdeen was that at one stage both routes converged. The North British and the Caledonian operated a joint route north of the Tay to St Vigean's Junction, north of Arbroath, which was straight, level and well suited to high-speed running. The lines then separated from St Vigean's Junction to Kinnaber, where the East and West Coast routes combined once again, this time running over track that was owned by the Caledonian, for the final leg of the journey to Aberdeen. Here again the North British line was poor. Not only was it steeply graded, but at the time it was still single-track, so even if a train was given priority, it still had to be slowed for the hand exchange of the tablets, not only at St Vigean's Junction, but also after the passing loops at Letham Grange, Inverkeilor, Lunan Bay and Montrose, before the final exchange at Kinnaber, where the tablet for the section was handed back. Even the most adept of firemen could not be expected to catch the tablets at more than 35mph, and often it was much slower. Given such a difficult line, any advantage to the East Coast route of a sixteen-mile saving in mileage between London and Aberdeen evaporated. Again, there was no attempt at the time to improve the route and double the track, although this was done in later years.

Some commentators began to speculate on competition between the east and West Coast companies to reach Aberdeen. In the case of the East Coast, this would be a three-company bid as the North British took over trains at Edinburgh, finally getting the rake of carriages away from the clutches of the NER, which still insisted on its loco-motives and drivers heading trains between Berwick and Edinburgh, even though this stretch was, of course, North British track.

* At one time Aberdeen was known as the 'Granite City' because of the stone used in its buildings, but in more recent times the 'Silvery City' has been used to present a more attractive and tempting image. Suffice to say that on a sunny day, even in mid-winter, the latter description is justified.

A hint of what was to come appeared, not in time for the busy summer timetable, but in October 1890, after the Forth Bridge had opened. There had been speculation about a new race, but this time Perth was seen as the favourite destination, especially as the Caledonian had opened a new Station Hotel, while others thought of Dundee or Aberdeen, or even Inverness. The latter was at the end of a long and demanding line with many single-track sections, and Inverness was smaller than Aberdeen or Dundee. Those who saw Perth as the most likely destination seemed to have their confidence in the fair city confirmed when the West Coast companies accelerated the 10.30am departure from Euston so that it reached Perth eighteen minutes earlier at 8.27pm instead of 8.45pm, while Dundee was twenty minutes quicker with an arrival at 9.15pm instead of 9.35. It seemed as if another 'race' was starting.

The speculation was not without foundation. What may have caught many unawares, when it did start, was that the trains chosen were not the crack day expresses, but the overnight sleepers, generally operated at a more leisurely and restful pace, partly for the comfort of the passengers and partly for economy in the use of coal, but also to ensure that departure and arrival times were convenient for the passengers.

In fact, the East Coast had already made the first move to celebrate, as it were, the opening of the Forth Bridge. Shortly afterwards, the East Coast companies brought the Aberdeen arrival of the 8.00pm from King's Cross forward from 8.55am to 8.15am. In response, the West Coast companies brought their 8.00pm departure from Euston, which had been reaching Aberdeen at 8.50am, forward to an 8.05am arrival. This was a significant improvement, made all the more important because the West Coast service was by far the more punctual, with better track throughout from Euston to Aberdeen. By contrast, the East Coast route not only had the drawbacks already mentioned north of Edinburgh, but the old Waverley Station was also deficient, being chaotic in a layout that was inimical to good working. As mentioned earlier, East Coast timekeeping left much to be desired, even between King's Cross and Edinburgh, but getting through Edinburgh and onwards to Aberdeen was yet another problem to add to the difficulties facing the route.

Despite these shortcomings, in 1891 the East Coast overnight arrival at Aberdeen was brought forward to 7.45am, cutting a further half-hour off the through journey time. This was followed by a further cut of ten minutes in 1893.

More than just the merest whiff of a new race was in the wind.

The West Coast companies then played their hand. When on time, the East Coast overnight train had connected with the Great North of Scotland Railway's Deeside express, which departed Aberdeen for Ballater at 7.50am. This was traffic denied the West Coast companies until, in June 1893, they persuaded the GNSR to put their departure back to 8.00am, and by tightening the schedule of the 8.00pm departure from Euston so that it reached Aberdeen at 7.50am, they were able to offer a connection onwards to Ballater. The East Coast companies were also in time for the connection, but, of course, the West Coast companies had the further advantage of superior timekeeping.

Throughout that summer, the East Coast retained its advantage of fifteen minutes over the West Coast, roughly in keeping with the shorter distance at around a mile-a-minute. As shown above, running to Aberdeen brought the East and West Coast companies into direct contact for the final stage of the journey.

'The change entailed very close running with the East Coast train,' explained George Neele. 'The signalman at Kinnaber Junction had daily anxiety as to the priority of passage of the two rival trains. Telegrams at Euston of the morning arrivals at Aberdeen were among the first tidings of the day's work.'

While most of the races were centred around the overnight trains running from Euston and King's Cross to Aberdeen, the first skirmish and a warning of things to come was with the day expresses, and started in 1893.

While relations between the two parties were, on the face of it, friendly*, certainly between Euston and King's Cross, there was another aspect to it. While the 1888 races to Edinburgh had involved the London & North Western and the Caledonian on the West Coast, and the Great Northern and the North Eastern on the East Coast, extending this rivalry through to Aberdeen entailed involving a third railway on the East Coast, the North British. Relationships north of the border between the Caledonian and the North British were not good. In contrast to 1888 when different termini about a mile apart in Edinburgh were used, the two railways had to use the same terminus in Aberdeen and, even worse, the same stretch of line between

---

*While it is not unknown in business for there to be friendly rivalry, especially amongst transport operators for whom safety is paramount, a competitive edge is always sought.

Kinnaber Junction and Aberdeen. Anyone working for the North British was inducted with a hatred of the Caledonian rather than a simple sense of rivalry, and the ill-feeling was returned. Some of the attitudes of the early days of the railways, when rival companies had their employees take action, such as that mentioned earlier at Havant, to undermine or embarrass their rivals, persisted.

Kinnaber Junction Holds the Key to Victory
This mattered, and it mattered a lot, because the signalbox at Kinnaber Junction was part of the Caledonian Railway. If the North British train was running late and the signalman at Kinnaber Junction checked the train to allow the Caledonian train to pass on time, goodwill was not simply strained but began to ebb away.

Not only the overnight sleepers were affected. As the rumblings that fresh races might be coming continued, the West Coast companies announced that from 1 January 1893, the 10.00am departure from Euston, due to arrive in Aberdeen at 10.55pm, would be brought forward to 10.25pm, just five minutes after the East Coast train. This meant that all was well if both trains presented at Kinnaber Junction on time, but the realities of railway operation meant that the earlier East Coast train could easily be late, so clashing with the West Coast train, or the West Coast train could be early. Even today, with the acceleration of a modern electric train, or, in the case of Aberdeen, a modern diesel train, stopping could delay a train for far longer than the actual period it was checked at a signal. In the days of steam, such signal checks were a far more serious matter, especially if the weather was wet, leaving the rails slippery. There was good reason for the 'daily anxiety' mentioned by George Neele.

Fortunately, there was another difference between the situation on the road to Aberdeen than had prevailed during the earlier races to Edinburgh. The Caledonian had to be aware well in advance of any changes made by either the East or West Coast companies, and the company's timetable planners realised the likelihood of conflict. The solution devised was highly unusual, as in the working timetable for 1 January a pass-to-pass time of six minutes was allocated for the 1.2 miles between Dubton and Kinnaber. On the face of it this was a generous four minutes of recovery time, but in practice what was intended was that the Dubton signalbox offered the train to Kinnaber at the time it was due to pass in the working timetable *whether the train had arrived or not*, but the competing North British train was not offered until it was actually passing Montrose. In this way, the North British train was blocked three nights out of four. Oddly, it took some time before the North British head office at Edinburgh Waverley realised what was going on. In fact, almost seven weeks elapsed before the North British actually observed what was happening and the general manager sent this memorandum to the other East Coast companies.

> This method of timing enabled the Caledonian Company's signalman at Kinnaber Junction to accept the Caledonian train some time before it actually reached Dubton, even though the North British train was then close to Kinnaber Junction, but this was not observed by the North British officials until February 16, 1893, when, on the North British train approaching Kinnaber Junction *three minutes* late, which Junction it would have passed, if its journey had not been interrupted, *four* minutes before the Caledonian train was due there; the North British train was stopped by signal while the Caledonian was allowed to come forward to the junction and proceed in front, whereby a further delay of *thirteen* minutes was caused to the North British train before it reached Aberdeen. On the following day, the North British train approached Kinnaber Junction on time, or *seven* minutes before the Caledonian train was due to pass, but it was again stopped by signal while the Caledonian was allowed to come forward to the Junction and again precede the North British train, which consequently lost *sixteen* minutes on the remainder of its journey to Aberdeen.

Here we have it in a nutshell, the strengths and weaknesses of the old pre-1923 railway. The strengths were the way in which companies could collaborate and provide long-distance trunk services that worked very well and provided a seamless service to the passenger and the shipper of goods, or freight as most of the railway companies termed it. The weaknesses were the way in which one company could behave in a blatantly partisan manner. It is not a case of allowing a late train to catch up to the detriment of a train running to schedule – until infrastructure and trains were separated in Great Britain, it was normal practice to ensure that a train running on time remained on time, even if a late running train was delayed further. It was a case of deliberately ensuring that a train running on time was delayed, and indeed could only remain on time if it passed Montrose early!

This point clearly hit home for the East Coast companies. The answer was clear. Once the train arrived from London at Edinburgh Waverley and was divided, instead of sending the Perth portion away first at 6.40pm and the Aberdeen portion away at 6.55pm, the Aberdeen portion went first at 6.40pm and the Perth portion followed at 6.50pm. This worked for a time at least, preventing any clash of interests or questions of priority at Kinnaber Junction.

The Caledonian was not long in revealing another ruse, this time at Perth and affecting the overnight 8.00pm departure from King's Cross. The 8.00pm from Euston had reached Perth at 5.55am, while that from King's Cross had arrived at 5.45am, at least until 31 May 1893. The Caledonian train that had originated at Euston continued its journey at 6.00am, so that passengers from King's Cross travelling to destinations such as Forfar and Brechin had a convenient connection. As the line was entirely Caledonian, it was not until sometime during May that the North British learnt, unofficially, of a plan to bring forward the departure of the Caledonian train to 5.45am, effectively ending the connection. Forewarned, the North British arranged to get their train into Perth at 5.40am, continuing the connection, if the train was on time, at least for those awake and alert enough to scramble from one train to the other in five minutes. When the Caledonian announced their change at the very last minute, the North British was able to counter by announcing their own change.

Inevitably, the person most at risk in this game-playing was the passenger, not because of any inherent risk to life or limb, but because of inconvenience, especially when connections were, if anything, more important than today. Services were, on the whole, less frequent then, and without the back up of motorized road transport. Not everyone had a telephone in their house, so letting anyone waiting for a passenger off the train know that a connection had been missed was another problem for the traveller on a long journey. Those waiting to welcome them had no idea of what the arrival time would be until they reached the station.

The North British move was in fact brilliant, as it was a minor adjustment that maintained a connection and yet reduced any suspicion of a betrayal on the part of a Caledonian official.

Ready for the 'Off'
In comparison with 1893, the following year was the calm before the storm. The first straw in the wind was the decision by the West Coast

companies that the 7.50am arrival at Aberdeen did not allow enough time for a reliable and comfortable connection with the GNSR train to Ballater. This was partly because the West Coast night trains were not as punctual as their day counterparts. So, from 1 June 1895, the West Coast overnight train was brought forward to arrive at Aberdeen at 7.40am. This did give the traveller onwards to Deeside extra time, but it also reopened the question of priority at Kinnaber Junction.

Faced with a renewed problem at Kinnaber Junction that could undo the good work that had been done earlier and make the East Coast connection with the Deeside train unreliable, the East Coast companies repeated what they had done earlier with the day trains, announcing that from 1 July 1895, the 8.00pm from London was scheduled to reach Aberdeen at 7.20am.

To achieve this meant that the North British had to have the collaboration of its East Coast partners, and break the 1888 agreement that prohibited any acceleration south of Edinburgh, on the grounds that it was no longer binding now that the rivalry with the West Coast for Edinburgh traffic had ended. Instead of the agreed eight and a half hours between London and Edinburgh, the schedule was cut to eight hours thirteen minutes.

This meant that for the first two weeks of July, the East Coast train was twenty minutes faster than its West Coast rival. What was worse for the West Coast companies was that throughout that period, the 8.00pm departure from Euston ran badly and was only on time at Aberdeen twice. For the rest of the time, the train was between five and thirty-five minutes late.

The Trains and their Locomotives

These were not the racing trains of 1888, with four or five carriages. The departures from Euston were usually of fifteen carriages and often as many as seventeen. Traffic and other delays meant that most of the hold-ups were south of the border, with trains arriving at Carlisle as much as twenty-eight minutes late. While many six-wheelers remained on the East Coast, with bogie carriages still rare, although becoming more usual for sleeping cars, the West Coast had been quicker in changing to eight-wheeled bogies, which offered a much more comfortable ride, but were also much heavier.

Locomotive power had also changed. South of the border, the North Western had in 1889 produced a three-cylinder compound locomotive,

Webb's *Teutonic*, the first of ten such locomotives with uncoupled 7ft driving wheels with improved valves and steam ports, and capable of 80mph. These were able to take heavier loads than the Precedent-class, although the lack of connecting rods meant that the driving wheels and the high and low-pressure cylinders were not synchro-nized, which could make starting interesting!

On the other side of the border, in some ways the Caledonian had made the least progress in locomotive design, with the Drummond 4–4–0 very much in evidence, both in the original form and in Lambie's development of the locomotive, in which boiler pressure was raised from 150lb per square inch to 160lb. Most obvious to an onlooker was the disappearance of the Caledonian's distinctive safety valve on the locomotive dome that immediately showed that these were Lambie locomotives, not Drummond, as otherwise the appear-ance and external dimensions were much the same.

On the North Eastern, Thomas Worsdell had been succeeded by his brother Wilson in 1890, who had for assistants the far-sighted Vincent Raven and the meticulous Walter Smith. His appointment was fol-lowed by a change of general manager when Henry Tennant was succeeded by George Gibb. This was to prove to be a highly competent and competitive quartet. The first fruit of the new regime was what was at the time Britain's most powerful steam locomotive, the new M-class 4–4–0, with the first being No. 1620. This appeared in 1892, but did not get a warm welcome. The new arrival was immediately criticized because it did not have a compound design, and in fact was usually described as a 'simple'. Changes were soon made and the fourth locomotive of the class was built as a two-cylinder compound. Nevertheless, these impressive locomotives for the day were soon nicknamed 'real-crushers'.

It may have seemed a retrograde step when Wilson started convert-ing his brother's successful J-class 4–2–2 singles, with their 7ft 7in driving wheels, from compound locomotives to 'simples', starting in 1895, but these proved to be easy running and economical in coal consumption. They are reputed to have been popular with footplate crews (especially firemen) and, no doubt, the management.

Moving north of the border once again, the North British was quickly becoming an operator of 4–4–0 locomotives, with the earliest being designed by Drummond before he was wooed away by the Caledonian, and the more recent the work of Matthew Holmes. The mainstay of this stable of locomotives was the 633-class, similar to the locomotives worked by the Caledonian in appearance and power. Lambie's increased boiler pressure propelled the Caledonian back into the lead. By contrast, the first work of Holmes on the large fleet of new locomotives needed to work the through expresses across the Forth and the Tay was to improve their appearance, including adopting a variant of Stirling's cut-away cab.

Aggressive Competition

In the spirit of aggressive competition, the West Coast companies decided to act without forewarning their rivals. On Monday, 15 July 1895, advertisements appeared in the morning newspapers and large blue posters were posted at Euston announcing that day's 8.00pm departure would reach Aberdeen at 7.00am the following day. The message was telegraphed down the line to ensure that there could be no doubt about the seriousness of good timekeeping. The message got through. This time there was no ancient single-wheeler rostered for the departure from Euston that night. Instead, two Precedent-class locomotives were allocated to the train, alternating between No. 749 *Mercury* and No. 394 *Eamont*, with *Mercury* used on the first night. These two handled the 8.00pm almost every evening for the next month, missing just four departures. The locomotives were crewed by the same team each time: *Mercury* had E. Holt as driver and A.T. Hewins as fireman, while *Eamont* had J. Daynes as driver and J. Stinson as fireman. The next morning the train arrived at Aberdeen not at 7.00am, but at 6.47am!

The first stage to Crewe had been three hours, as with the 10.00am of 1888, but this was steadily reduced to two hours fifty-three minutes. *Mercury* arrived at Crewe on time that first night, with a load of 130 tons. Here locomotives were changed and another Precedent-class, No. 790 *Hardwicke*, with Driver B. 'Big Ben' Robinson and Fireman W. Wolstencroft, took the train forward non-stop to Carlisle (there were no refreshment stops on the night sleepers), covering 141.1 miles in 163 minutes and arriving twelve minutes early. *Hardwicke* was to remain the locomotive for this section for the first ten days of the new timetable, with the relief crew being Driver P. Howman and Fireman J. Harrison, taking alternate nights with Robinson and Wolstencroft. At Carlisle there was another change of locomotives and a handover to the Caledonian, which provided a Drummond 4–4–0, No. 90. There was no hanging around and the train was given the 'right-away' at 1.54am.

Apart from on two days, the Caledonian also divided the duty for the section between Carlisle and Perth between two drivers, although it seems that the firemen varied. The drivers were Archibald 'Baldie' Crooks with No. 90, and Tom Robinson with No. 78. Further north, for the final section between Perth and Aberdeen, a link of six drivers was allocated to the service. On the first night, it was John Soutar, with one of the most up-to-date Lambie 4–4–0s, while the other five drivers used Drummond 4–4–0s.

When the train arrived at Aberdeen, no mention was made of the early departures, and for a while the East Coast team were allowed to think that the time had been made up between the last call at Forfar and Aberdeen, but suspicions grew as the distance was hardly enough to allow such an early arrival.

The race was on.

Racing in Earnest

Having advertised the new schedule in that morning's newspapers, there had been no delay in the news getting to King's Cross. Sir Henry Oakley, General Manager of the Great Northern, telegraphed J. Conacher, his opposite number at the North British: 'See North Western notice of further acceleration of night trains. What can you do in response? Gibb is in London and will be here this morning. Wire reply.' 'Gibb' was Sir George Gibb, General Manager of the North Eastern Railway.

Oakley and Gibb did meet and the two men quickly agreed that something must be done to remain competitive, and that there should be a meeting of the superintendents of the three East Coast companies that night at York, which all could reach in the time available. The telegram sounded more like a command than a communication between equals, possibly because Oakley was irritated by the slowness of a reply from Conacher. He simply said: 'Scotch train service. Have seen Gibb, and arranged for Superintendents [of the Line] to meet tonight at York. Please instruct Deuchars to attend.'

This provoked a response at 2.45pm. 'Your telegram. Deuchars is to go to York by train leaving here at 2.50pm. As he requires to be back here tomorrow morning, I trust you have made arrangements for meeting of Superintendents taking place tonight.'

Conacher's delay in replying had been caused by him waiting for reports from his managers on just what could be done. 'Your three telegrams of today,' telegraphed Conacher at 4.55pm:

If you can take fifteen minutes less by the 8.00pm to Edinburgh we can save another fifteen here and on the way to Aberdeen, arriving 6.50am. The 10.00pm train cannot be accelerated to get to Aberdeen before 10.40 without running a new train throughout from Edinburgh, and I do not think traffic will justify our increasing the expense. If, however, as a matter of policy it is necessary to show West Coast that persistence in their present moves will not secure the advantage in time to them I shall be willing to join in accelerating the train also for present season if you and Gibb will secure us against absolute loss. In that case we should reach Aberdeen at 9.25. Deuchars has gone to York with instructions to this effect.

The result of the meeting at York and the behind-the-scenes work at King's Cross, York and Waverley, was that the East Coast companies were able to advertise their 8.00pm overnight train as arriving in Aberdeen at 6.45am from Monday 22 July, a significant improvement on the previously advertised arrival time of 7.20am.

Meanwhile, the first week's running of the West Coast train had seen arrivals at Aberdeen that were thirteen, thirty-nine, five, nine, ten and twenty-one minutes early. In fact, if the first night's performance had been impressive, even startling, that of the second night, 16/17 July, had been breathtaking. Howman brought *Hardwicke* into Carlisle fifteen minutes early, and the change of locomotives took just five minutes. Tom Robinson then took the train away, driving No. 78, and, despite a call at Stirling, reached Perth twenty-eight minutes early, running 150 miles in 167 minutes. Driver William Kerr with Drummond No. 70 took over for the remaining ninety miles to Aberdeen, with a booked call at Forfar, but took just ninety-eight minutes instead of the booked 110 minutes, so that the train arrived at Aberdeen at 6.21am, thirty-nine minutes early.

The East Coast companies had no details of the timings at intermediate stops on the West Coast train, and this was a weakness in their planning of any response. As it happened, on the first day the East Coast train reached Aberdeen on time at 6.45am, only to find the West Coast train sitting there, having arrived at 6.39am. Unknown to the East Coast companies, the West Coast had stolen yet another march on them by changing the working timetable to give an arrival at 6.35am from 23 July.

The reason for the East Coast companies being ignorant of the moves being made by their rivals was that the public timetable was unchanged, although regular travellers and others interested in the railway scene were well aware of what was going on. Strangely, no one amongst the three East Coast companies had thought to book a place aboard the train for someone from the office of their super-intendent of the line. The senior members of this elite group would have been well known to the West Coast companies, but a relative junior, bright and ambitious, could have done the job. Even placing observers at key points could have provided the much-needed infor-mation.

It was not that the railway companies were averse to a little spying, as Mr F.G. Cockman, of Bedford, recalled:

My father-in-law, Mr A.E.B. Mason, commenced his railway career in the booking office at Little Bytham in 1889, and duly pro-ceeded to the Passenger Manager's office at King's Cross. In 1895, during the competitive running, he was instructed to go to Euston daily as a 'spy' and to keep his eyes and ears open on what the 'enemy' proposed to do next day. No doubt many G.N. officials were detailed for this duty, but it goes to show how keen the com-petition was. He had particularly to find out what the schedule was being cut to, until schedule times were abandoned, and I believe he was able to assist the G.N.R. by ascertaining the L.N.W. Plans.

Nevertheless, on this occasion, the truth was recognized very quickly. A one-off performance could have been the work of a single driver, although in all reason the distance a single driver covered would have made this difficult. That it was not a one-off effort but a sustained campaign became all too clear the following morning when the 8.00pm from Euston was brought into Aberdeen by the Caledonian at 6.30am on 24 July.

The race was already being noticed and reported on by *The Railway News*, in an item in the edition of Saturday, 27 July, headed 'The Race to Aberdeen'.

SHAREHOLDERS in the East and West Coast routes will not read with the same satisfaction as the travelling public of the race to

Aberdeen, commenced with this summer season. The race to Edinburgh in 1888 was the outcome of a claim by the West Coast companies to be allowed a position of equality for Edinburgh traffic, and that claim the West Coast made good, for since September, 1888, the trains by both routes have run in the identical time of 8½ hours. Emboldened by success, the West Coast companies are now claiming equality in a similar manner in the traffic to Perth, and more especially to Aberdeen, to which points till now the East Coast route has been tacitly conceded an advance of something like 10 to 20 minutes, and this claim the East Coast companies, who have invested more than two millions sterling in the Forth Bridge in order to get the better of their rivals, seem prepared to resist to the uttermost.

An Inverness correspondent to the *Times* wrote:

to an outsider the two combatants seem pretty evenly matched to Aberdeen, which is the real objective point in the present movement. The East Coast route is 17 miles shorter, the distances being 523 and 540 miles respectively. The East Coast has also the advantage of better gradients. On the other hand, a good many miles of it are run over single line, a fact that implies not only the certainty of slacks every few miles, but a possibility of more serious delays. Moreover, nearly 40 miles is over the Caledonian Company's road, and under such circumstances, signals have an awkward knack of going unexpectedly to danger. Again, the North-Western has a real advantage in its system of water troughs, from which the engines can replenish their tender tanks without stopping. Finally, a complete understanding is easier between only two companies than where three are concerned. But it is time to come to the actual fight.

For a long time past both routes here have had an 8 p.m. express to Aberdeen , the West Coast train arriving at 7.50 and that by the East Coast 15 minutes earlier. The West Coast had also a 10 p.m. train which reached Aberdeen at 2 o'clock the following afternoon. Suddenly, on June 22 last, the West Coast companies advertised – and without giving previous private notice, as is said to be usual in similar circumstances – that from and after July 1 the 8 o'clock would be accelerated ten minutes to Aberdeen, while the 10 p.m. would be quickened no less than two hours. The East Coast companies instantly took up the challenge, and replied by advertising an acceleration of their 8 o'clock train by a quarter of an hour, while an entirely new train was put on at 10 o'clock, reaching Aberdeen a clear hour in front of its rival. The West Coast waited a fortnight and then returned the ball. They took off a further 40 minutes from the time of the 8 o'clock and 80 minutes from the time of the 10 o'clock, so bringing in both of these trains in front of the East Coast. The final stage of the combat so far was reached on Monday night, when the East Coast took yet another quarter of an hour off the time of the 8 o'clock and an hour-and-a-quarter off the time of the 10 o'clock. The advertised times accordingly now are: Leave London, 8 p.m., reach Aberdeen, East Coast, 6.45 a.m., West Coast 7 a.m.; leave London 10 p.m., reach Aberdeen, East Coast 9.45 a.m., West Coast 10.40 a.m. So far, therefore, the East Coast would seem to have kept in front.

But advertised times are one thing and actual times quite another, and this morning when the East Coast train ran into Aberdeen station half a minute before time it was only to find that the West Coast passengers had been there six minutes already; and, indeed this was not the best West Coast performance. For one day last week their train came in at 6.21, an inclusive speed of over 52 miles per hour throughout. If, on the other hand, the East Coast similarly reckoned is under 49, sufficient explanation is no doubt to be found in the fact that instructions have been given that the booked times are to be strictly adhered to. Further, it should be said that whereas the West Coast train consists of only six eight-wheel vehicles with a total weight of about 130 tons, the East Coast load is eleven vehicles weighing not less than 175 tons. Moreover the West Coast has fewer stops. In the 385 miles from Euston to Law Junction near Glasgow there are only two inter-mediate stops at Crewe and Carlisle respectively, and in the whole distance to Aberdeen there are only six. The East Coast has seven, Grantham, York, Newcastle, Grant's House (for water only), Edinburgh, Dundee, Arbroath. On the whole the fight seems a very evenly balanced one, and it is with no surprise that I read in this morning's Aberdeen paper that in future the West Coast propose to take 6.35 a.m. as their regular time of arrival, of course assuming, which is most improbable, that the East Coast continues to be satisfied with 6.45. Railway men will be interested to know that the North-Western are working their train with engines of the well-known President-class, now more than twenty years old.

That the public appreciate the efforts made in this race to Aberdeen on their behalf is evident from the fact that at both Euston and King's Cross all the sleeping berths by the 8 and 10 p.m. trains for Scotland were engaged on Friday, and we presume are filled every night.

Once again, Oakley wired Conacher, stressing that the West Coast companies were determined to offer the shortest journey and the earliest arrival times. It is clear at this stage that while the Great Northern was concerned about one train, the North British were taking a far wider view of the service between London and Scotland as a whole. There was sense in this, not least because raising the standard overall was far wiser and more attractive to the travelling public, and also reduced the chances of heavy bookings for one train while other departures were overlooked. Conacher also seems to have been aware of the dangers of a schedule that was too tight, and not robust enough to cope with the delays that could arise without warning. The old steam railway was in some ways more robust than the modern railway, as lighter trains and the lack of unsprung weight on a steam locomotive, unlike its diesel or electric counterpart, meant that broken rails were rare. However, bearings did overheat and mist or fog was a menace that would take many decades to overcome. The North-East of England and Edinburgh were prone to heavy sea mists, known as the haar in Edinburgh and the sea fret in Northumberland, while London fog was notorious.

'Your telegram,' Conacher wired Oakley:

We could reach Aberdeen at 6.25. Should not like to attempt earlier arrival meanwhile. Now that West Coast have advertised* their arrival 6.35 I think that we had better accelerate the 10 o'clock also and get both trains into Bradshaw and other guides for August. What can you do in improving 10 o'clock train. We can take twenty minutes off time Edinburgh to Aberdeen. With corresponding acceleration south of Edinburgh we could make connection with the express to Ballater and 9.30 express to Elgin and Inverness.

---

*This was incorrect as the arrival hadn't been advertised, but it was well known nevertheless.

Oakley did not reply immediately but waited until the next day, 25 July, after discussing the matter with the GNR's chairman, the Hon. W.L. Jackson. He wanted to know what the NBR board would think of an approach to Lord Stalbridge, chairman of the LNWR, over the whole question of racing. Conacher telegraphed his chairman, the Marquis of Tweeddale, who happened to be in London, for his opinion on what to do next. This need to consult and the relative slowness of the telegraph meant that decision-making was slower and more protracted than it would be today, but Tweeddale was in no doubt as to what to do.

'My opinion is our best policy is to beat them at any cost and having done it proceed [to] remonstrate,' Lord Tweeddale replied. 'Stalbridge has always complained of the speed being too great and has suggested more moderate speed, but the present is deliberate and well-considered attempt to show what they can do, and we should strive to win.'

This decision was conveyed to Oakley and, on 29 July, the East Coast schedule was amended in line with Conacher's recommendations for a ten hour twenty-five minute schedule between London King's Cross and Aberdeen, so that the train arrived at 6.25. The working timetable allowed a total running time of ten hours three minutes, with the last three minutes being the time between the ticket platform* at Aberdeen and arrival in the terminus.

On the first night of operation, the North British succeeded in beating the time between Edinburgh and Dundee of seventy-three minutes for the difficult 59.2 miles by one and a half minutes despite a heavy load of 150 tons. Aberdeen was reached at 6.23, knocking a couple of minutes off the schedule. What frustration, disappointment and anti-climax must have been felt for those aboard to find the West Coast train already sitting there, having arrived at 6.06am. The West Coast had brought arrival forward in the working timetable to 6.20am!

In fact, the East Coast could have done even better that night. At King's Cross the train had been about 180 tons, but this presented no problems for the GNR locomotives. First of these, for the run from King's Cross to Grantham, was a new 7ft 6in single, No. 874, which was replaced at Grantham by an 8ft single, No. 1002. Just over three

---

*In the early days of the railway, with non-corridor carriages, tickets were checked at the station prior to the terminus, and if there wasn't one close enough, a stop was made at a specially-built ticket platform for this purpose.

minutes were saved on the run to Grantham and a further ninety-five seconds onwards to York. This is where the two setbacks occurred. Not only was a private saloon attached, bringing the load up to around 195 tons, but the NER's allocated locomotive was not up to the weight of the train, a 4–2–2 J-class, No. 1522, that had just been converted to a two-cylinder simple. No.1522 took an extra six minutes between York and Darlington, although with a slight check only another minute was lost onwards to Newcastle.

Leaving Newcastle seven minutes late, the train was double-headed with No. 1621, an M-class single, and another single, No. 1525, and most of the lost time was recovered by the time Edinburgh Waverley was reached. Despite leaving Edinburgh ninety seconds late behind a new 6ft 6in 4–4–0 Holmes locomotive, the train arrived early at Dundee, and ran ahead of time from Dundee to Arbroath.

Even had the schedule been maintained between York and Newcastle, the arrival at Aberdeen would still have been ten minutes behind that of the West Coast train.

The official schedules remained the same for the next month as the railways were in the busy period leading up to the 'Glorious Twelfth' of August, the start of the shooting season. Both companies kept the timetables, with the West Coast even maintaining that the arrival at Aberdeen of the 8.00pm from Euston was still 7.00am!

What, for many, was more important than the overall time was the question of punctuality. The twenty-four nights between 29 July and 18 August showed the West Coast companies to be far superior. On 30 July, their '7.00am arrival' actually reached Aberdeen at 5.59, and the worst performance was on 18 August when the train arrived at 6.23am; the only occasion on which it failed to meet the time specified in the working timetable.

The West Coast seems to have allowed its drivers and officers on the route considerable discretion. On 9 August, *Eamont* was struggling with a load of 'equal to 13'; Driver Daynes realized that he was losing time and stopped at Rugby for assistance. A second locomotive of the same class was attached and the train managed to make up some time to arrive at Crewe just three minutes late. This was the only instance of double-heading south of Crewe, but when the load exceeded 'equal to 11½', double-heading was provided with two Lady of the Lake-class 2–2–2s, No. 610 *Princess Royal* and No. 622 *Prince Alfred*, assigned for piloting the racing train.

By contrast, the East Coast train was early on only four occasions, with the best being eight minutes early on 18 August, and on time on only two occasions. The other eighteen arrivals were up to forty minutes late, as on 4 August, and on another four occasions arrival was between twenty and twenty-nine minutes late. The Great Northern, by contrast, at no time double-headed the East Coast racing train and was the only company not to use this tactic, although, in the company's favour, the time lost always seems to have been north of York, where the terrain became more difficult once Berwick-on-Tweed was passed.

Running was monitored by the three enthusiastic letter-writers mentioned earlier, and they were joined by a New Zealand journalist, Charles Rous-Marten, editor of the *New Zealand Times*, commissioned by his government to undertake a survey of Britain's railways. According to O.S. Nock:

> Rous-Marten had all the flair of a professional journalist for vivid description, and for feats of endurance when first-class copy was to be had. He never varied his picturesque attire – black frock coat and tall hat – and it was shown to memorable advantage one memorable morning when he had travelled to Aberdeen by the 8.00pm from King's Cross. In order to pursue his ordinary duties he was anxious to get back to London as soon as possible; the 'flyer' was coasting into the station just as the up express for Edinburgh was starting, and racing across the platform with coat tails flying he just managed it. He was assisted in by an astonished guard, who remarked: 'Ye'll no' be makin' a long stay in Aberdeen the mor-r-n'.

Back in the News

By this time, the race had come to the attention of the London newspapers. Each evening's departure was watched by a large crowd of onlookers, while others chose vantage points along the line. Each side had its adherents, passionate about one company or another, equally passionate about one locomotive design or another. Some favoured the large single driving wheel, while others preferred compound locomotives, still in their infancy. Neither of these two groups would have known that while a compound locomotive has more grip in theory, the leading pair of wheels depresses the track slightly so that the second pair does not have the same amount of grip. On the other hand, as the need for power grew, the single-wheeler was doomed because of its ultimate limitations. At King's Cross, the main expresses used to leave from Platform 6, but the 8.00pm always used Platform 9 as it was the one used by the George Hudson trains to the north, and it was retained for the races because it had the least curve in its exit line of any of the platforms and so locomotives were less likely to slip.

Anecdotal accounts tell of young railwaymen returning long after their working day had finished to see the trains depart, or of a young child of just nine-and-a-half years being allowed up at 1.00am to see the North Western train dashing into Carlisle: a rare treat for a Victorian child who was expected to be in bed early, and stay there!

Press interest threw light on the subterfuge or even downright sabotage at Kinnaber Junction. This is one account:

> The following story is told by the Caledonian Railway officials in connection with the railway race: Both trains they declare, reached Kinnaber Junction where the two routes meet, at precisely the same time. On Thursday morning, 22nd, ult, the trains from Arbroath, on the East Coast route and Forfar, on the Western line, were sighted by the signalman in the Kinnaber box at an identical moment. The signalman is a Caledonian man belonging, of course, to the West Coast route, and one would naturally expect that he would have let his own train through first. By a rare act of chivalry, however, he gave priority to the East Coast train, which consequently arrived in Aberdeen first. This story is right enough, no doubt, but we should like to hear it from the lips of other than Caledonian officials.

The cynicism of the journalist was well-placed. One Caledonian fireman was claimed to have told how on one occasion they were signalled through Kinnaber, and on arrival at the junction found the East Coast train standing, checked by a signal, to allow them through. Some versions of this story tell of a brawl between the two engine crews when the East Coast train eventually arrived at Aberdeen.

Then there were rumours, with the professors at St Andrew's University circulating a story that on one occasion, after crossing the Forth Bridge, the North British locomotive had pulled its train at 200 miles per hour! Others, which sound more realistic, were that while the curvature of the line was adequate for the speeds actually achieved, the pressure of the fast train moved the track out of alignment by as much as three inches at Cupar in Fife. Certainly, the permanent way men were out every night to ensure that the track on both routes was in tip-top condition, and nowhere more so than on the sharply curved and steeply graded line through Fife between the Forth and Tay bridges.

Is certain, however, that whatever the commercial advantage of higher speeds, at the time this was not always appreciated by the passengers, many of whom were riding in six-wheeled carriages, without corridors and with little padding in their upholstery. A Mr Swaine from Sussex recalled travelling from Euston to Aberdeen overnight in such a carriage, with a very rough ride. He was not at all surprised to arrive in Aberdeen fifty minutes early.

D.A. Guild, of Elgin, tells the story of an elderly passenger who definitely did not appreciate the race:

> I remember the stern comments of some of the grave and revered seniors, who were appalled that such dangerous goings-on should be allowed. I remember one pleasing tale of an old gentleman we knew who was going north by Perth. The driver must have been feeling his oats. Anyhow, coming down from Crieff Junction (later known as Gleneagles) the train started to shift a bit. This got on the old boy's nerves. After a while he could stand it no longer, and in the face of the threatened penalties he decided to pull the communication cord. However at that time the communication cord only functioned on the right hand side of the compartment facing in the direction of travel. There might be a cord on the left hand side, and often was, but it was not connected up. In his agitation the old boy got hold of the wrong cord. He pulled and pulled until he got to the end of the rope, and then gave it up in despair. He arrived at the north end of the tunnel in a state of tremendous agitation with his compartment festooned with communication cord. He confided his woes to the ticket collector at Perth, and all the consolation he got was to be told that he was adjectively lucky it had happened that way or else he would have been fined £5.

It was not only the passengers who were becoming concerned, or shall we say agitated?

Sticking his neck out considerably, a Caledonian pointsman wrote to the *Railway Herald*. This prompted a lengthy reply from a Mr W.D.J. Edwards of Chelsea in the issue of 15 August 1895:

> To state the case briefly, it would be difficult to measure accurately the advantage to the shareholders of the Company.

Certainly at first sight it does not seem consistent with economy to have, as was the case in the famous race in August 1888, five separate expresses on the West Coast to different parts of Scotland within two hours, where two or three trains as far as Carstairs Junction would have been sufficient, with three Midland trains and five Great Northern expresses on different routes, but with the same objective points, when one or two respectively might have sufficed for the greater part of the journey. But each company has its prestige to maintain, otherwise public support is withdrawn and if it be suggested that amalgamation might result in more economy to the shareholder, the reply is that the British public have a most steady inclination in favour of competitive railways. Moreover, progress requires competition.

Again, permanent acceleration follows upon such contests and thus railway travelling is encouraged. When the journey to Glasgow or Edinburgh took, as was the case twenty years ago, even in the fastest train, and in third-class trains several hours more, a journey demanded almost heroism; whereas now, when 8½ hours suffices, even for third-class passengers too, there is no hesitancy, the journey is less serious, and the number of passengers has increased enormously. At the same time, economy in working becomes, with keener competition, a necessity, so that ingenuity towards this end is stimulated. Thus there is a measure of permanent good even to the shareholders, which cannot be accurately estimated.

That there is advantage to the general public there is no doubt. The 1888 race gave ample proof of this.

Then again, the advantages to the profession are almost self-evident. In the first place it has been found absolutely necessary to have the best of permanent way, and strong, well-built bogie carriages. As to the permanent way, the London & North Western have recently introduced 60-ft rails, and although some consider the length unwieldy, the reduction in the number of joints may prove of advantage. The fact that the great speed attained is scarcely appreciable in the carriages at once attests their smooth-running qualities. The comfort and convenience in most cases introduced by the introduction of the corridor arrangement, are luxurious as compared with the old carriages.

The racing trains, it is true, are comparatively light. Those on the Aberdeen service just now consist of from 6 to 11 eight-wheel bogies carriages, the train weight being from 130 to 175 tons, but the speeds got with the heaviest trains show that even to Aberdeen the speed recorded is not abnormally great. The 8½ hours run to Edinburgh was made with similar light trains, but now the mid-day dining train, leaving Euston at 2.00pm and King's Cross at 2.20pm covers the distance to Edinburgh in 8½ hours easily. These trains of themselves weigh 360 tons on the West Coast route and on the East Coast route 300 tons – very much more than the racing trains of 1888. It is true that on some occasions, when the traffic is heavy, two engines are used, but as a rule one engine takes the load, the coal consumption being from 30lb to 31lb for compound, and 33lb to 34lb for non-compound locomotives – much having been gleaned from these performances in reference to locomotive running.

This was a succinct summing up of the advantages of the races and of competition between railway companies.

Chapter 9

The Race is Back On!

Having taken a break from racing until 18 August, albeit with strong competition to meet or exceed the schedules, there was renewed interest as the end of the month drew near. At a meeting on 13 August, officers from the three East Coast companies met at York, under the chairmanship of J. Welburn of the NER. It must have been a large meeting as each company sent its superintendent of the line and locomotive superintendent, plus others. The minutes of the meeting record that:

It was agreed that from the 19th to the 23rd instant the following be the accelerated times of the 8.00pm train from King's Cross:

King's Cross	*dep.*	8.00 pm
York	*arr.*	11.18 pm
	dep.	11.23 pm
Newcastle	*arr.*	12.43 am
	dep.	12.46 am
Berwick	*pass*	1.55 am
Edinburgh	*arr.*	2.55 am
	dep.	2.58 am
Dundee	*arr.*	4.08 am
	dep.	4.10 am
Arbroath	*arr.*	4.30 am
	dep.	4.32 am
Kinnaber Junction	*pass*	4.56 am
Aberdeen	*arr.*	5.40 am

The foregoing times are subject to alteration if the Great Northern Company can tomorrow see their way to further acceleration.

That the train be made up of the following vehicles: Aberdeen brake van; third-class carriage (corridor); sleeping carriage; composite carriage (corridor); third-class carriage (corridor); North British brake van.

The train not to exceed eight vehicles under any circumstance whilst it is running at the accelerated times ... It was the feeling of the meeting that the accelerated times of the train should not be advertised.

The concluding statement said it all. To announce the new schedule was to hold it a hostage to fortune. The West Coast had been setting the pace that summer and the East Coast, despite its proven ability to produce a new schedule and implement it almost as quickly, had been left trailing behind. The problems at Kinnaber Junction were a major cause of its poor timekeeping, but not the only one.

The pressure was heaviest on the North Eastern. Up until this time, the NER had left most of the acceleration to the GNR and the NBR, but the decision of 13 August meant that the NER had to provide the fastest start-to-stop schedule of the entire journey between King's Cross and Aberdeen, covering the 80.6 miles between York and Newcastle in eighty minutes, a fraction over 60mph and the magic mile-a-minute. By contrast, the GNR's run from King's Cross to Grantham would take 109 minutes for 105.5 miles, an average speed of 58.1mph, and from Grantham to York the 82.7 miles would take eighty-six minutes, an average of 57.7mph. Further north, the arduous 124.4 miles between Newcastle and Edinburgh, also performed by the NER, was allowed 129 minutes. Rather than going for an absolute maximum speed, the intention was to raise the average by making faster starts, with a fine example being the allowance of just eleven minutes for the 11.2 miles between York and Alne, giving an average speed over this section of 61.1mph!

In the circular to staff advising them of the new schedules, it was made clear that the train would only convey passengers north to Dundee and Aberdeen, with those for intermediate stations having to change at Dundee, requiring a duplicate of the 8.00pm departure to serve passengers for those stations that would be missed or from which an early departure would be permitted. The train would not under any circumstances stop to set down passengers at any station which it was not timed to do, nor would it carry any fish traffic. This was followed by a further instruction in heavy type:

PARTICULAR ATTENTION MUST BE PAID TO THE PROMPT TELEGRAPHING OF THE RUNNING OF THE EXPRESS PASSENGER TRAINS REFERRED TO HEREIN, AND THE MARGINS HITHERTO OBSERVED BETWEEN TRAINS OF

LESS IMPORTANCE AND THE 8 P.M. EXPRESS TRAIN FROM KINGS CROSS MUST UNTIL FURTHER NOTICE BE INCREASED TO THE EXTENT OF NOT LESS THAN TEN MINUTES, AND ALL CONCERNED ARE TO UNDERSTAND DISTINCTLY THAT THE LINE MUST BE KEPT ABSOLUTELY CLEAR FOR THESE TRAINS TO RUN.

This was it. There was to be no doubt whatsoever that the train had priority and other trains were to be kept clear of it, regardless of the impact on their schedule. The magnitude of what the East Coast companies were attempting can all too easily be underestimated more than a century later when train speeds are more than twice those of the 1890s. Over the 523½ miles from King's Cross to Aberdeen the average speed was to be 54mph including stops to change locomotives. The train would arrive a full twenty-six minutes ahead of the West Coast train, which meant that the East Coast companies were hoping that the delays at Kinnaber Junction would not occur. There were other supporting instructions issued, including a letter dated 14 August and marked 'Very Important' from Patrick Stirling to his district superintendent, F. Rouse, at Peterborough, headed '8.0 P.M. DOWN SCOTCH EXPRESS.'

Dear Sir,
The L.&N.W. Co. have expressed their intention to reach Aberdeen before us. This of course we cannot permit and arrangements are being made by this Company and the N.E. and N.B. Railways to accelerate the speed of the above train commencing on Monday next.
We must reach York at 11.15pm. The load will not exceed 6 whenever possible to keep it to that number and 7 will be the maximum in every case. The N.E. Company have undertaken to run their share of the distance at high speed, over 60½ miles per hour York to Newcastle and the N.B. also.
Please put your men on their mettle!
Acknowledge receipt of this preliminary notice and oblige.
Yours truly,
P. STIRLING

This was laying it on the line, but many in the Locomotive Department had their doubts about the new schedule, even though the GNR had once been the world's fastest railway. The doubters were not confined to the Locomotive Department, leading the General Manager, Sir Henry Oakley, to write to Stirling. This, of course, was the inevitable outcome of leaving such an important decision to departmental heads rather than the general management of the three companies. On 15 August, Stirling replied to Oakley.

Dear Sir,
I am in receipt of yours of the 14th inst. In reference to the acceleration of the 8.00 p.m. train to Aberdeen and in view of the competitive nature of the traffic and seeing what the L. & N.W. Co are doing I am quite willing to meet the demand made by the Traffic Department, i.e. to engage (wind and weather and other adverse contingencies permitting) to work the 8.0 p.m. train between London and York in 3 hours and 18 minutes.

The load however must be kept down to 6 whenever possible and should never exceed 7 vehicles. This Mr Matthewman stipulated for in his interview with Mr Alexander yesterday. Under such conditions I have no doubt of its feasibility.

I may tell you that on the 15th inst. with 9 vehicles on we arrived at York at 11.23 p.m. and on the 7th with 10 on we got there at 11.22 p.m.

Yours truly,
P. STIRLING
P.S. (We will not stick at 8 however)

The letter is slightly ambiguous in the postscript, which suggests that eight vehicles might be allowable despite having insisted that seven would be the absolute maximum and six the usual figure. Stirling then departed for Scarborough for his summer holiday, but his rest and relaxation was to be disturbed when J.W. Matthewman, Stirling's clerk and chief accountant, was sent after him with a further letter. This led to yet another letter on 16 August, marked 'Private', on this occasion from Matthewman, at Doncaster, to Rouse at Peterborough, and which for the first time was officially headed as concerning the 'race' to Aberdeen.

Dear Sir,
                    RACE TO ABERDEEN
I went down to Scarboro yesterday to consult Mr Stirling in reference to a communication from Sir Henry Oakley upon the subject of the race to Aberdeen, and he desired me to again ask

you to impress upon your drivers the absolute need there is that we should get into York at the time booked, viz. 11.18 , or a few minutes earlier if possible.

The drivers must not study economy of fuel in the race, but must beat the North Western, whatever they may burn in the way of fuel of the best selected quality.

Tell them please that this will be fully allowed for in the distribution of premiums, and further, Mr Stirling thinks it will be well to give the men some extra pecuniary allowance, such as ¼ of a day's pay, whenever they arrive on time, or in any other way by *douceur* or otherwise that may best secure the end in view. What do you recommend please?

He has undertaken to the General Manager to beat everybody else, and he relies on you and all the staff to leave no stone unturned to do this.

There is great anxiety also I may say that the other trains, viz. The 8.30 and 10 o'clock as well as the duplicate of the race train should be punctually worked.

Yours truly,
J.W. MATTHEWMAN

Unfortunately there is no copy of Rouse's reply. It seems that he may have been defending his men, while the proposal that coal consumption did not matter probably went very much against the grain. Either way, Matthewman did receive a letter from Rouse dated 17 August to which a reply was sent on 19 August, the very day of the new timetable. This was short and to the point, indicating that the GNR's footplatemen had not been doing their best.

Dear Sir,
ACCELERATION OF 8.0 P.M. DOWN EXPRESS
of 17th inst.
I am obliged for the above. I may point out that in the opinion of the Traffic Department the men had *not* been doing well because they had failed to recover the time lost by relayers, station business, signals, etc. and the suggestion that an extra payment should be made as an inducement to the men to do their very best regardless of fuel and premium was put forward in consequence.

Yours truly,
J.W. MATTHEWMAN

The secret was not confined to the senior officers in the three East Coast companies, as the newspaper letter-writers were in on it, and Norman Macdonald actually travelled up to London to catch the racer, accompanied by W.M. Gilbert, chief of staff of *The Scotsman*. Once in London, they were joined by the Rev. W.J. Scott, Charles Rous-Marten, W.M. Acworth and one of the leading railway photographers of the day, Percy Caldecott. Inevitably, they all had their stopwatches.

Despite originally being reluctant to publicise what was happening, on the first night the East Coast companies seemed anxious to court publicity. A sleeper was put at the disposal of the little band of enthusiasts and journalists, but Scott noted in 1897 in his leaflet *Kinnaber* that their free passes only extended to Kinnaber Junction and that they had to pay full fare for the final dash over the Caledonian and into Aberdeen. He recalled:

> Even now, two full years after, it is hard to write about it in cold blood. Beforehand: the reckoning of mileage, and working out of intermediate speeds, when the working notices came into one's hands. Then the chat and chaff with the traffic officers, who wavered between drinking delight of battle with their peers and feeling (or making believe to feel) ashamed of the whole thing as not practical 'business'. This usually ended with a vain effort to keep a certain superintendent away from the engine, that he might not give restraining instructions to the driver – then the whistle, and the train and our chronographs begin moving together ... a night of long drawn out excitement when our hopes were constantly raised by fine running, only to be dashed again by signal stops or 'waiting for time', while through good fortune or ill the fifths of seconds ticked off remorselessly, and the friendly conductor stayed us with hot coffee or comforted us with bread and butter.

Clearly, these were good friends of the East Coast companies. Bizarrely, Cockshott seems to have been inclined to press caution on the drivers, urging them to be attentive to their work. Was he one of those who had doubts about the wisdom of racing? The doubters weren't confined to the Locomotive Department, including many drivers who had been brought up to consider economy in the use of coal, perhaps remembering their days as firemen, but also included a number in the management team at King's Cross. It is also clear that the East Coast companies were not going to follow the West Coast companies in completely disregarding the timetable. Instead, they had changed it by not admitting passengers at certain stations to the train. Naively, they placed their hopes on the train being on time at Dundee to beat the Caledonian.

At King's Cross, the train consisted of just six carriages, as specified by the meeting on 13 August and emphasised since then by Stirling. The locomotive was an 8ft single-wheeler, No. 668, from Peterborough's New England depot. The driver, J. Falkinder, from the same shed, has been described as taciturn and silent to the point of unfriendliness, solid and safe, not one to enjoy a race. Not for nothing had Stirling suggested extra pay. The whistle blew and the train departed on time, but time was lost on the run to Hatfield, and then there was a permanent way slack around Welwyn. After this, however, No. 668 showed what she could do, averaging 68½mph over the 33.9 miles between Knebworth and Huntingdon. At Peterborough they were ahead of the best timings achieved in 1888 and at Grantham they were three minutes early, having taken just 105 minutes fifty-five seconds from King's Cross. At Grantham, the locomotives were changed and another 8ft single-wheeler, No. 775, took over. Although built in 1886, the locomotive soon showed a fine performance, keeping the set timings over the sections to Newark, and then running on to Doncaster with an average speed of 66mph. Onwards to York, and despite a slack at Selby the run from Grantham to York was completed in the record time of seventy-nine and a half minutes, with a start-to-stop average of 62.3mph, with arrival at York nine minutes early.

The locomotive change at York took four minutes, with the single-wheeler replaced by No. 1624, a Worsdell M-class 4–4–0, but although the schedule called for the 22.2 miles to Thirsk to be completed in just twenty-one minutes, the locomotive took twenty-two minutes forty-six seconds to pass Thirsk. Then one of those many minor incidents that can affect the best railway timetabling occurred, as a train in front had a tail lamp not working and the 8.00pm from King's Cross had to be checked at what was then Dalton Junction, but later named Eryholme, while the defective lamp was replaced. The lost time could not be recovered, but the run from York to Newcastle took eighty-three minutes forty-five seconds, arriving at 12.43am, six minutes early.

The train ran into Newcastle over the High Level Bridge, with the locomotive coming to a stand facing towards Carlisle. The replacement locomotive, NER No. 1621, backed down behind her and touched buffers almost as soon as the down train had stopped, and in two and a half minutes the train was on her way again. On the run to Berwick-on-Tweed, little if any time was gained, and some believe that the driver was worried about conserving water, as the East Coast route lacked water troughs at the time and he would have had to stop to take on water. The run of 124.4 miles to Edinburgh was lengthy for a single tankful of water, although those on the NER carried 3,940 gallons.

After passing Grantshouse, approached from the south by a long climb, the driver began to relax and let his locomotive have her head. As Scott later wrote:

> But such a change for the better now befalls us as we spin off the remaining 41¼ miles in just 38 minutes, dropping down by Cockburnspath at 80 m.p.h. easing very little for Dunbar, with a terrific spurt by Portobello, No. 1621 fairly charges up the Carlton Tunnel steep and we pull up in Waverley at a trifle before 2.45 a.m., 6 hours 44 minutes 50 seconds for the more than 393 miles from London, or 42 minutes better than the 'Race to Edinburgh' best.

In fact there was more to it than this, and the train and its passengers had a brief brush with danger and even death. It was another forty years before Macdonald let the cat out of the bag by telling the whole story.

> The last week of the 'Race' was nearly the death of a group of famous and infamous folk *i.e.* the Rev. W.J. Scott, Sir William Acworth, C. Rous-Marten, Percy Caldecott, W.M. Gilbert and myself. It fell on this-wise. My East Coast friends (N.E.R., N.B.R., and G.N.R.) always put on a 'sleeper' for my party when any new spurt effort came to the birth. Till I got the N.E.R. to build the first transverse-berthed 'sleeper' these were made up of cabins of two beds placed longitudinally, entered from a passage across the car.
>
> At Portobello (Edinburgh) there was a very bad S-curve with our usual half-hearted British elevation, ending in a high bridge across a wide road.
>
> At Inveresk Rous-Marten, with his four split watches (one in each hand and one in each trousers pocket) called '82mph'. I said, 'If these two* big Worsdells don't slack off we will be thrown

---

* In fact, only one Worsdell was being used, stressing how important it is to get one's account down while the memory is still fresh.

through the windows, even if we stay on the rails at the Portobello S.' I quickly got the six into the cross passage, where we jammed our legs and arms against the walls, myself at one window and Rous-Marten at the other. Just before the curves he called '81½', and I yelled, 'Look out!' as we struck it. The whole of them were thrown on to me, and we collapsed as does a Rugby maul, and in the next second we were hurled up again and on to the top of C. R-M. In his dry Dutch way he was heard to say, 'We would have made bonnie raspberry jam in that Duddington Road!' When we arrived into Waverley out of the Carlton Tunnel (after a mile of 1:78 up) we were doing about 64 m.p.h. and Acworth remarked, 'Thank goodness we are working Westinghouse and not vacuum, and that Waverley* is very long!'

They had arrived at Edinburgh Waverley ten minutes early, and this was followed by a locomotive change in just two minutes, with a Holmes 4–4–0 No. 293 attached to the train. Expecting a fast departure, they were disappointed by the lack of movement, and the truth dawned: they were being kept waiting for their scheduled departure time. The North British, while anxious to score a victory over their rivals the Caledonian, nevertheless had a schedule to keep to, although in the end someone relented and sent the train ahead two minutes early.

For those aboard, eight hard-won minutes had been lost. As if to compensate, the driver of No. 293 raced away and took just eleven minutes to the Forth Bridge and then a further 11.3 miles to Burntisland took just twelve minutes thirty-five seconds, giving an average speed of 53.8mph. The 39.1 miles from Waverley to Ladybank Junction took just forty-two minutes fifty-five seconds, despite the many sharp curves on this stretch of line. Dundee was reached in sixty-four minutes fifteen seconds for the 59.2 miles. Despite this, the locomotive had to take water at Dundee, and so left two and a half minutes early, although the correspondent for *The Times*, below, differed on this matter. Some surmise that, for the rest of the run, a different driver had taken over, but no one can be sure as the North British did not note the name of the driver on any of the records kept

*Waverley is a very long station with terminating platforms in the centre for trains from both east and west, and in between them the station offices. The terminating platforms are flanked by through platforms that can take two full-length trains at a time.

during the races. The relatively easy and straight run to Arbroath took a disappointing twenty minutes forty-five seconds, but the 16¼ miles onwards to Kinnaber took just nineteen minutes forty-five seconds despite having to slow six times to change tablets for the single-track sections. The result was that by the time they sailed past Kinnaber Junction the train was eight and a half minutes early. The average speed that far was 55.2mph, but had the train not been checked at Dalton and had it been allowed to leave the stations as soon as it was ready, the speed would have been 58.6mph. Kinnaber was passed thirty-five minutes earlier than the best the West Coast had achieved at the time. The final eighteen miles to the ticket platform at Aberdeen were run in nineteen minutes forty seconds.

The ticket platform was manned by Caledonian inspectors. They took great satisfaction in telling the passengers aboard the 'racer' that their West Coast rival had passed into the terminus sixteen minutes previously! The average speed for the Euston train had been 58.4mph start-to-stop.

Such was the public interest that *The Times* had a special correspondent aboard who had no qualms in describing the frustration felt by the officious station work.

The train, which weighed about 105 tons throughout, was timed to reach Grantham, 105¼ miles, at 9.49, it in fact got there at 9.47. For the 82¾ miles thence to York 86 min. were allowed and only 80 taken – a most magnificent performance for unvarying but never excessive speed. We left York, accordingly, full 10 min. in front of time, and booked to run the next 80½ miles in exactly 80 min. But in railway matters, alas! though officers propose signalmen dispose, and no less than three signal checks, the last an actual full stop between York and Darlington, resulted in our only reaching Newcastle at 12.37, 6 min. in front of time. Off again in 2 min. we covered 124½ miles to Edinburgh in 126 min., a fine run, which gave us once more 10 min. in hand. Our time here was exactly 2.45, 6¾ hours from London, a record that will take, I fancy, a good deal of beating. The record of 1883 was 7 hours 27 min., but that, it is fair to say, included a long stop for lunch at York. But at Edinburgh there occurred an inexplicable mistake which shattered all our high hopes, and, as the result proved, led to our being thoroughly beaten into Aberdeen. From Edinburgh forward the train was an extra or special followed by an ordinary train in the times as given by 'Bradshaw'. Yet for some inscrutable reason it had been decreed by the authorities that we must not leave until the booked time of 2.58. For eleven weary minutes, accordingly, engine and passengers fumed till at 2.56, the station clock being fortunately two minutes wrong, we started afresh. We gained six minutes on our booked time to Dundee, only once more to kick our heels for eight minutes at the platform. Off again at 4.8, we picked up another eight minutes en route, and finally reached Aberdeen at 5.30 to find that, as has been said already, the West Coast train had been there a quarter of an hour. Had our iron horse not been pulled at Edinburgh and Dundee, we should have run a dead heat to the judge's box at Kinnaber.

Whether the North Western at Euston had prior warning that the East Coast was planning an attempt on the record to Aberdeen that night, or it was some sixth sense or just the simple desire to try and do better, there had been considerable effort put into the run of 19/20 August, and an air of excitement and expectation on the departure platform at Euston.

The previous Friday, 16 August, the 8.00pm departure had been worked by a 4–4–0 compound, the Teutonic-class No. 1307 *Coptic*, for the first time since 21 July. The driver was 'Peter the Dandy' Clow of Rugby, who forsook the normal working clothes of an engine driver, the peaked cap, blue jacket and overalls, and instead was dressed in a black tailcoat, tall hat and a well-laundered white shirt. He was known to enjoy a contest and owned a profitable bookmakers as well as running a public house in Rugby during his spare time.

Despite the West Coast companies still advertising a 7.00am arrival at Aberdeen for the night of 19/20 August, the choice of Driver Clow once again showed that the competitive spirit had returned after the start of the shooting season. The light load was another factor that would have given the game away to the knowledgeable observer. Just four bogie carriages, weighing in total about 95 tons, were to be taken to Crewe by No. 1309 *Adriatic*, and Peter Crow took just 157 minutes to cover the 158.1 miles. The conventional layout at Crewe meant that the locomotive change needed four minutes to allow for uncoupling and the first locomotive to run safely out of the way before the replacement could back onto the train and be coupled to it. The new driver was W.J. Phillips with the 6ft 6in 'Jumbo' No. 1683 *Sisyphus*, whose performance was certainly no less than that of Crow, taking just 140 minutes start-to-stop for the 141.1 miles from Crewe to Carlisle, Shap notwithstanding.

Once again the Caledonian rostered Tom Robinson and a Drummond 4–4–0, who once again did not disappoint by running the 150 miles from Carlisle to Perth in 155 minutes despite a call at Stirling. A similar locomotive, No. 70, under the charge of Driver William Kerr, took over at Perth, and ran the last 89.8 miles to Aberdeen in just eighty-nine minutes, despite the call at the ticket platform, giving a start-to-stop average of 60.65mph. Sadly, there are no logs of this impressive performance, and no thrilling eye-witness accounts.

The East Coast observers proved to be thoroughly biased in their collections. Scott saw a 'moral triumph' for the East Coast as defeat was due to the 'stern resolve of the North British officers not to allow any "before time" departures', although he contradicted himself by publishing details that showed that the train had been allowed away from Waverley two and a half minutes early and from Dundee two minutes early. The total delays at both stations after the train was ready totalled thirteen minutes and the West Coast had won by sixteen minutes. It would indeed have been close run but for the signal check at Dalton, aka Eryholme, and the peculiar arrangements put in place at Kinnaber Junction could well have played a deciding role had not these delays been incurred.

Rous-Marten seemed to be angry rather than just disappointed in his account, published in *The Engineer*:

> But then 20 minutes had been absolutely wasted in delays at Dalton, Edinburgh and Dundee, in the first case by a blundering signal stop, and in the other by mere idling at stations long after all was in readiness for the start. These blunders were doubtless due to a misunderstanding, but they were grave blunders nevertheless, and resulted in making a present of an easy victory to the rival route.

'Easy victory' seems unfair for the West Coast's hard work and excellent planning.

The view of the man in the street of these performances was interesting. 'By mid-August,' one wrote, 'Aberdonians were rubbing their eyes and wondering if at this rate the granite city was going to become a sort of northern suburb of London!'

The day that dawned with the defeat of the East Coast companies was also the one that had been chosen for a further conference, this time in Edinburgh. This had been set to review progress, but, of course, it was more an opportunity for a post mortem and even recriminations. Naturally, none of this came out in the minutes of the meeting, which simply noted that all present had agreed that an earlier departure from Edinburgh than 2.58am should be arranged, and that the staff involved should be instructed to keep the line ahead clear for ten minutes on the Great Northern, and fifteen minutes on the North Eastern and North British. The train would also be retimed to leave Edinburgh at 2.43am; Dundee at 3.50am after a 3.48am arrival; pass Arbroath at 4.09am and Kinnaber Junction at 4.31am; so as to arrive at Aberdeen at 5.13am. That the NBR was to some extent taking the blame for failure was simply noted as 'the arrangement being that N.B. Company should run as much before these times as possible.' The new working timetable was to remain in force until and including 23 August, but could be continued depending on the agreement of the three general managers.

Chapter 10

The Final Phase

After such a disappointment, the situation was that the East Coast companies had finally given up any hope of sticking to advertised departure times and had joined their West Coast rivals in sweeping aside any obstacle to progress, at least as far as possible on a busy railway. The working timetables for the departures at 8.00pm on Tuesday, 20 August 1895 showed arrivals at Aberdeen at 5.35am for the West Coast companies and 5.13am for the East Coast companies. It was clear that this was to be the final push. Neither company could guarantee ever-faster services, especially with autumn and winter approaching, as poor visibility, heavy rain, high winds and, of course, snow would affect even their pre-race timings. Given the events of the past month, there was great excitement amongst the crowds who had flocked to Euston and King's Cross.

Even today, some of the timings would be tight, notably the schedule of sixty-five minutes between Edinburgh and Dundee, including a 40mph limit over the Forth Bridge even then, and of course the gradients and curves through Fife, although, of course, nothing runs non-stop between these two cities now.

On the West Coast, the Caledonian made no further changes in their working timetable after 19 August, but the North Western tightened the schedule each night, although Euston to Crewe was not as fast as Crewe to Carlisle, despite the fearful ascent of Shap.

At Euston, it was the same locomotive, *Adriatic*, again, but the LNWR double-crewed its locomotives and this time it was not 'Peter the Dandy' driving but his opposite number, R. Walker. Walker started very well, running the 97.1 miles to Nuneaton in ninety-three and a half minutes, much of it with an average speed over sections well in excess of 60mph. One of the great advantages possessed by the West Coast companies was the availability of water pick-up troughs, still to be installed on the East Coast, but there seems to have been a problem with the equipment on the night of 20/21 August, as the train had to stop at Stafford for water, which took what must have seemed like an agonisingly slow three and a half minutes before he was on his way again. Despite this, Walker reached Crewe in 156¼ minutes, a whole minute earlier than the previous night when, of course, there had been no such problem with the water pick-up equipment.

The locomotive change at Crewe completed, there came the fastest part of the journey onwards to Carlisle with the locomotive No. 790, *Hardwicke*, with Driver B.L. Robinson and Fireman Wolstencroft. Disappointingly, on this occasion, with 134 minutes booked for the 141 miles to Carlisle, they actually took 135¾ minutes. This was despite some extremely fast running for the day with an average speed start-to-pass between Crewe and Preston of 65.6mph.

At Carlisle came the handover to a Caledonian locomotive and crew, on this occasion No. 90 with Baldie Crooks driving. The 117¾ miles onwards to Stirling, with the ascent of Beattock, took exactly two hours, giving an average speed of 59mph. Stirling was reached in six hours fifty-seven and a half minutes, arriving at 2.17½am. Staying just ninety seconds at Stirling, the train then covered the thirty-three miles to Perth in thirty-four minutes start-to-stop.

Meanwhile, at King's Cross locomotive No. 668 was the locomotive once again and J. Falkinder once again was the driver. This seems a curious choice, as he was known to be reliable, but hardly a 'racer'. This became all too clear when, despite incentives to push his locomotive as hard as he could, he took 106 minutes for the relatively easy run to Grantham and even between Hatfield and Peterborough his average speed was just 64mph. The reputation of the GNR was saved when the locomotives were changed at Peterborough and the next crew arrived at York at 11.07pm, having saved a valuable eleven minutes against the schedule. The NER crew and locomotive taking over the train at York worked in the same spirit, running the 80.6 miles from York to Newcastle in seventy-seven and a half minutes, giving an average speed of 62.3mph, but even so Newcastle was reached at 12.29½ pm, only seven minutes ahead of the previous night. Macdonald had gone in person to complain to Deuchars at Waverley after the previous night's frantic run through Portobello, with a speed restriction no higher than 15mph, and this may have affected performance between Newcastle and Edinburgh. Berwick-on-Tweed was passed in sixty-eight minutes despite it being just 66.9 miles, and this was before the more difficult section north of the border. It took sixty-three and a half minutes for the 57.5 miles from passing Berwick to coming to a stand at Waverley, against just fifty-seven minutes the previous night. The result was that the East Coast express did not reach Edinburgh Waverley until 2.42am, just thirteen minutes ahead of the previous night's schedule.

Whatever had been said at the meeting during the afternoon of 20 August, this time there was no question that the station staff at Waverley were intent on getting the train away as quickly as possible. It took just two minutes to get the North Eastern locomotive and a brake van off the train and a North British locomotive coupled on to it. Leaving Edinburgh at 2.44am, the train arrived at Dundee thirty seconds before 3.45am and was away within ninety seconds. At 4.21am, it was a mile south of Montrose, and if it could pass Montrose before the West Coast train passed Dubton Junction, the train would have priority at Kinnaber Junction.

The trouble was that once again the East Coast companies seemed to have a driver without the determination to win or the understanding of what was at stake. The West Coast train, headed by Lambie 4–4–0 No. 17, was running between Coupar Angus and Forfar at between 70mph and 75mph – no accurate log exists for a more precise measurement – but the East Coast train was running along the Angus coast on equally good and level alignment at just above 60mph. The North British driver, seemingly contrary to the last, pounded up the gradients after each check for a tablet for a single-line section, but relaxed once on the level.

After Lunan Bay, with the early daybreak of a Scottish summer, those aboard the East Coast train could see across country the smoke of another train running fast. The West Coast train reached Dubton at 4.21am; the East Coast train reached Montrose at 4.22am.

The existence of Kinnaber Junction meant that for the racing trains, the rest of the journey was an anti-climax for the train that came second at Kinnaber. Aberdeen may have been the objective, the end of the journey, but Kinnaber decreed who came first. There were no prizes or kudos for coming second.

It was left to the West Coast train to run on to the ticket platform at Aberdeen in 33¾ minutes for the 37.9 miles, setting a new record for the journey between London and Aberdeen of eight hours fifty-eight minutes, arriving at 4.48am. The East Coast train didn't even try to make haste after being checked at Kinnaber Junction, and arrived at Aberdeen at 5.11am. Despite the shorter distance over the East Coast, an average speed of 61.5mph start-to-stop on the West Coast against an average of 59.2mph on the East Coast more than compensated for the fact that the West Coast train had to travel 501.7 miles against 485.7 miles for the East Coast train. All this despite the unscheduled stop for water at Stafford, although for the final stretch the 'train' lost two of its carriages at Perth and consisted of just two carriages and a fish van to steady the train, but of course the East Coast train had also been shortened at Edinburgh with the detaching of the brake van.

None of this cheating by the two companies by running unrealistically short trains would have been apparent to those reading a report of the race that appeared in the *Standard* on 22 August:

> There was again a fierce contest on the East and West Coast Routes yesterday morning in the great railway race to the North. Both trains started punctually at eight o'clock on Tuesday night from Euston and Kings Cross, and some splendid running on both routes was accomplished. The West Coast train, however, gained the day, steaming into Aberdeen Station at 4.58 yesterday morning, the journey of 540 miles having been accomplished in 8 hours 58 minutes. Several spurts were run at 64 miles an hour. The East Coast train did not arrive until 5.11 which, however, beats all previous records on this route by 21 minutes. Both trains were well filled with passengers. It will be seen that the West Coast train covered the entire distance at the rate of 60 miles an hour with two minutes to spare.

It was not surprising that both trains were 'well filled' with passengers given the much shortened rake. The news item continued:

> With regard to the complaint that such rapid travelling produces a sensation of nausea, it may be mentioned that officials at Euston have received from a passenger who travelled by Tuesday night's train a telegram saying that the progress of the train was so smooth and comfortable that passengers could hardly realise the fact that they were travelling at a higher rate of speed than by ordinary train.

It is easy to cast blame on the North British driver as so many have done. He may well not have had much experience of fast running and been concerned about a derailment. This is where the East Coast companies failed. They did not seem to select drivers with a known reputation for fast running. The choice of Falkinder for the run to Grantham was a mistake. Was this man simply stubborn, or was he being insubordinate or just plain bloody-minded? He could have got the train off to a flying start and, once clear of the King's Cross tunnels, used the relatively easy running on the southernmost stretch to gain time. For the two successive nights, the more difficult stretch between Newcastle and Edinburgh seems to have been tackled by two drivers who were the complete opposite of one another. The first was reckless in running at very high speed over the difficult section passing Portobello, but the second showed excessive caution.

Of course, Falkinder may well have been showing his resentment at being given a train to drive that was hardly commercial, lacking sufficient accommodation to pay its way, while the arrival at Aberdeen was at an hour when there would be a wait for connections or for hotels to have staff other than the night porter to serve the hungry arrivals looking for breakfast after a shortened but often rough journey.

Finally, let us remember that the locomotives of the day did not have speedometers, and greater dependence was put upon the driver to judge what would be the safe speed for any stretch of track than is the case today. Only the strictest of speed restrictions was posted.

Fighting Back

To their credit, the East Coast companies were determined not to sit back and let the West Coast become the 'fastest route to Aberdeen'. This would have been humiliating, as the East Coast route was sixteen miles shorter. Prestige was at stake, and more than just prestige: hard cash from paying customers. The North British took the lead on this occasion.

'I again urge your lightening the train from Kings Cross,' Conacher wired Sir Henry Oakley on the morning of 21 August. He continued:

There is too much room in the train as now made up and if lightened as I suggest we might get to Kinnaber first and so keep ahead. West Coast train to Aberdeen this morning consisted of only two carriages and a fish truck to steady it.
Reply.

Oakley responded late afternoon to say that the traffic for the 8.00pm would be carefully watched, and that the load would be reduced wherever practicable.

By this time, interest had reawakened. Even on 19 August intermediate stations such as Newcastle Central had been empty, but not only did newspapers now position reporters at locomotive-changing stations, but vast crowds also assembled in the middle of the night.

The departure of 8.00pm on 21 August from Euston did not show any real gain in speed over the previous evening, with 'Peter the Dandy' Crow back as driver, but despite running non-stop to Crewe, he arrived only a minute earlier than Walker had achieved. No. 1213 *The Queen*, driven by W.J. Phillips, took over and covered the 141 miles from Crewe to Carlisle in 135 minutes, arriving at 12.53am and leaving at 12.56am in the care of the Caledonian Railway's No. 78, once again driven by Tom Robinson. This was when the race came alive again. Robinson covered the 117.8 miles from Carlisle to Stirling in 114 minutes, stopping for two minutes before steaming away again to take thirty-four minutes for the thirty-three miles to Perth, as on the previous evening. He had contributed to a record run between Euston and Stirling of 410 minutes for 416.9 miles start-to-stop, and at Perth the train arrived at 3.26am, the earliest achieved so far in the races.

Between King's Cross and Newcastle, the East Coast train also set a new record after clipping a further six minutes off the time between King's Cross and York, with an average of 62.7mph as far as Grantham, and then an average of 65.3mph onwards to York. These impressive figures were undermined by needing four minutes for the engine change at Grantham, and the same again at York, reached in three hours one minute from King's Cross. At York, an M-class, No. 1621 yet again, was attached and taken forward by Driver Turner and Fireman Elijah Hodgson, but despite relatively easy running they passed Thirsk at 22.2 miles in twenty-two and a half minutes, and towards Darlington the speed averaged 66mph, but seemed to have eased off by Durham so that the 66.1 miles from York took sixty-six and a half minutes. It was not until they reached the Team Valley that any racing spirit seemed to arise, and some have described the run past Gateshead and over the High Level Bridge into Newcastle as 'hair-raising'. Hodgson later maintained that this was necessary to impress their fellow footplatemen at the shed. True, they had managed the fourteen and a half miles into Newcastle in just twelve minutes, but on arrival at the station they had gained just a minute on the previous night's run from York, and overall the arrival was just five minutes better from King's Cross.

A further M-class, also already used on the races, No. 1620, driven by Robert Nicholson, said to be 'safer on the ground than on a locomotive footplate', came on at Newcastle with his fireman Tom Blades, and the change was sufficiently slick, according to a newspaper account, that it was cheered by the crowds on the platform, and the train steamed away to further cheers and the waving of handkerchiefs.

At last, the race was now on again!

Despite the curves at Morpeth and Alnmouth Junction, it took just thirty-three and a half minutes to pass Alnmouth, 34.8 miles away. A large crowd had assembled at Berwick-on-Tweed, where a speed restriction of just 5mph applied, so when the crowds saw the loco-motive coming tearing across the Royal Border Bridge, they scattered in fear of what might happen. The 66.9 miles from Berwick to Newcastle was covered in exactly one hour, and then over the difficult stretch to Dunbar an average of more than 60mph was maintained, before running along the Lothian coast at an average speed of 74mph with 78.8mph attained from Drem to Longniddry. One can only surmise that the Portobello section was taken with as little fear as on the night of 19/20 August, for the start-to-stop average for the 124.4 miles from Newcastle to Edinburgh was taken at an average speed of 66.2mph, taking just 113 minutes to arrive at 2.19am, so that the train arrived no less than eighteen minutes ahead of the previous night's run. The start-to-stop average from King's Cross was 62.2mph.

There was no fuss or delay at Edinburgh Waverley. The train was on its way again at 2.21am, twenty-three minutes ahead of the previous night. Now it was down to the North British, which so far had shown itself capable of some astonishing running over indifferent sections but, equally, of indifferent running over excellent sections. This time the North British did rather better, once again using Holmes's 4–4–0 locomotive No. 293 between Edinburgh and Dundee, reached in fifty-nine minutes, and then No. 262 from Dundee to Aberdeen. Although only a further thirty seconds was cut from the previous night's schedule, the East Coast train swept past Kinnaber Junction unchecked at 4.02½am, while the West Coast train followed at 4.17am. The Aberdeen ticket platform, so often the first source of bad news, was reached at 4.38am and the station itself at 4.40am. The train had covered 523.5 miles in 520 minutes, including stops and engine changes.

The East Coast companies had covered themselves in glory.

It was the morning for the West Coast companies to have the sour taste of defeat, even though their train had set a record for the run from Euston, when it arrived fourteen minutes later, of 539.8 miles in 534 minutes.

Shall We or Shan't We?

What to do next? That was the question that exercised the minds of the East Coast companies' managements. Obviously, it was long before the advent of the mobile phone, but even though landline telephones were available, railway company managements were reluctant to use them and in any case long-distance lines were often not that good. It was not just tradition that led them to use the relatively slow and clumsy telegraph, although of course the nation's telegraph system was largely based on the systems used by the railway companies and merged to create a national system when the 'wires' were nationalized in 1868. There was certainly no such facility as a 'conference call' on the telephones. Management decision-making at the time was far slower than today, but it also bred managers who had to use their initiative, unable to check every decision with their superiors.

The use of the telegraph did have the advantage that every proposal, every counter-proposal or objection, and every decision, was actually on record.

Ideally, the East Coast managers would have liked another conference. This was impossible. J. Conacher was in Aberdeen, away from his office in Edinburgh but, of course, best placed to savour the victory. Sir Henry Oakley was at his office at King's Cross, but the North Eastern's Sir George Gibb was on holiday, ironically in Scotland, staying at the Highland Railway's new hotel at Dornoch, a few miles north of Inverness. Conacher made the first move. He telegraphed Oakley at 9.00am:

> After this morning's achievement I think we ought tonight to revert to advertised time, making another effort later on if West Coast do better. There is a feeling here that rivalry has gone far enough already and I think that we might rest on the position gained unless again challenged when we can choose our own time for another effort. Have wired Gibb also. Shall be here all day.

Unfortunately Conacher did not mention that he was in Aberdeen, so the replies from Gibb and Oakley went to Edinburgh Waverley and had to be retransmitted to Aberdeen. This wasn't done until early afternoon. Both the other general managers were opposed to stopping just then.

'I think we ought to continue to shew our friends the hopelessness of their effort,' wired Oakley. 'Stopping now would be commented on. Please reply.' 'Having made record this morning my opinion in favour of continuing racing to this week,' wired Gibb, 'best policy to be able to prove that except this week we have worked our trains not as racers but under ordinary traffic conditions.'

So, while both men wanted to continue, they wanted to do so under different arrangements. In short, three general managers had three different views. This was not surprising. Conacher replied:

> You were repeated from Edinburgh. There are so many chances against our repeating last night's performance tonight and tomorrow night, especially as everything depends on reaching Kinnaber first, that I hesitate to risk spoiling it. If however you think otherwise I agree, but if you can do even better it ought to be done as West Coast will be sure to make great efforts tonight.

There was sound logic in all three positions. Let's stop racing as we have won and face up to the fact that it had to be a one-off that might not work again, was in essence the North British position. Stop now and people will think that it was just a one-off could be the opinion of his two colleagues, but they actually differed, as Oakley wanted to prove that the East Coast the fastest route, while Gibb wanted to show that they could also produce fast and reliable full trains, obviously at a slower pace. It was the first view that prevailed after Oakley raised the matter with his chairman, who perhaps also consulted other directors of the Great Northern.

'Gibb suggests we continue this week,' Oakley wired Conacher at 1.50pm after discussing the situation with his chairman. 'Have told you propose ceasing tonight. Feeling of directors here that we should cease having shewn what we can do. Reply now.'

Conacher replied an hour later:

> Your second telegram received. Am glad your directors agree to view expressed in my first telegram. I think it the safest course and most dignified. Wire here whether it is the 6.25 arrival going back to and I will instruct our people. Details can be settled by Superintendents.

The Railway News for Saturday, 24 August, was quite clear on the matter.

> We are informed by the respective managers of the Great Northern and North-Western companies, that the race to Aberdeen on the East and West Coast routes has ceased, at all events

for the present. The record time rests with the West Coast service, but the general running to which the companies revert leaves the East Coast route with an advantage of thirty-five minutes. The London and North-Western officials declare themselves content to have demonstrated that they could successfully 'cut' the time, and the Great Northern Railway is content to retain a slight lead on its ordinary running, so that honours may be declared easy ... At the ordinary accelerated speed, the Great Northern Company expects to be able to run ten, eleven, or even twelve heavy coaches, and to make all the usual stoppages.

It was indeed to be the 6.25am arrival. The decision was undoubtedly transmitted to all concerned by telegraph, but Sir Henry Oakley also took the opportunity later that day to write a letter to Conacher.

Dear Sir,
With reference to your telegrams today, I have obtained the authority of my Directors to revert to the advertised time of 6.25, and have instructed Mr Alexander accordingly. I received a telegram from York that the Chairman of the North Eastern wished the published times to be adhered. In the face of such a consensus of opinion, I of course waive my own predilections, which I confess would have been to have held on until the West Coast abandoned their senseless practice of running a train of 3 or 4 carriages.

The speed at which we ran last night was not higher than we run daily with our expresses from Yorkshire and Manchester, the only difference being that the lightening of the train to 6 carriages enabled us to run uphill almost as fast as we could run down. I did not, and do not, feel that there was any risk in the performance. However, as the decision is come to, it shall be loyally carried out.
Yours faithfully,
(*signed*) H. OAKLEY

The newspapers were not happy at the ending of what had become, to them, so exciting. They were, of course, always reporting a day late, as the arrival at Aberdeen, no matter how early, was too late for that day's morning newspapers to report. Even more unhappy, having paid their fares, were those passengers wishing to be part of the excitement.

The *Westminster Gazette* also interviewed the railway managements. The leading official of the London & North Western said:

We don't admit that we're racing at all. We only claim that it's possible for us to arrive in Aberdeen at the same time as the trains of the East Coast Railway, and that this is brought about not by uncomfortable running in any way, but owing principally to the fact that we have on this line water troughs between the rails. These water troughs, which, at certain points along the line, extend for two or three hundred yards between the rails, enable water to be taken up into the tank when the train is running at full speed.

The Great Northern official claimed that:

We have by 17 miles the shortest route to Aberdeen, by 8 miles the shortest to Edinburgh, and I think it will be admitted that our line has the easiest gradients. Our position is briefly this – that we can run to Edinburgh, Perth and Aberdeen in the same or less time than the West Coast at a lower rate of speed. Speed is almost entirely a matter of load. If the London & North-Western come down to a hand-cart behind their engine they might reach Aberdeen appreciably earlier than they do now. It's a very much easier matter, for example, to work a train of five or six vehicles at 55 miles an hour than a train of twelve or fifteen vehicles at 50 miles an hour. We try to maintain a high average of speed in good ordinary trains, and our working at present is distinctly an ordinary working. We are not now running, nor have we run during the competition, a single additional train. We have made no difference in the mileage of traffic. The 8.00pm train would be about 120 tons, the 8.10 train about 180 tons. The engine is one of Stirling's. There's nothing very special about it. We change engines at every station we stop at, as grit and what not gets in and hinders efficiency. As a matter of fact, the London and North-Western are running four vehicles. We stop at Grantham, York and Newcastle; not so much for water, but that the train may be examined – wheels, axles and so on. We attach great importance to that. I've no doubt we might run to York without stopping for water, but we prefer to stop at Grantham for a thorough exam-ination of the train. About twelve miles of the North British is single. We're going to double that. How many vehicles did the

London and North-Western take to Aberdeen? Our information is that they arrived at Aberdeen with two passenger vehicles and a fish van. We arrived with thirty-five passengers, and the West Coast train with twelve. Our train ran throughout with six vehicles. You may take it that it's quite the exception if the East Coast doesn't take six carriages on to Aberdeen. It may even be more than that. It's seldom less. We have orders tonight for nearly half the accommodation of the train.

Nevertheless, just as the East Coast and West Coast had kept their racing plans secret, the East Coast was in no hurry to let the West Coast know about the cancellation of the races, at least not until too late, when journalists waiting for the departure of the 8.00am train from King's Cross received the news. There was no such disappointment at Euston, as it became clear that the train, with just three carriages, was clearly a 'racer'. The *Yorkshire Post* carried the story the next day:

Euston station was the scene of much excitement about eight o'clock last night, a considerable number of spectators having arrived to give the West Coast train a 'send off'. The officials were determined if possible to wipe out the defeat sustained on the previous night, when their rivals won by 15 minutes. The train consisted of three large bogie carriages, which were fairly well filled with passengers, some of whom were visibly suffering from suppressed excitement, as though on the eve of doing great things. The driver of the train had received instructions to make the best time possible, and one facetious youth who was seeing a party of friends off seized upon it as the basis for some lugubrious predictions, and earnest appeal to take insurance tickets. As the clock indicated the hour of departure the whistle was blown, and the Aberdeen express steamed out of the station amid a chorus if hearty wishes for a safe and speedy journey.

The weather that night was very bad with one of the worst thunderstorms in living memory accompanied by torrential rain. Heavy rain meant poor visibility and slippery track. Despite this, *Adriatic* made a good getaway and was soon pounding along and set a new record for the 158¼ miles from London to Crewe, reached in two hours twenty-eight minutes, with an average speed of 64mph. It took just two minutes to change locomotives at Crewe, where once again

Hardwicke, with Driver Ben Robinson and Fireman Wolstencroft, took over for the run to Carlisle. Only a small gain was made on the speed of 19/20 August as far as Preston, taking 45¾ minutes as opposed to forty-six and a half minutes on the earlier occasion for the fifty-one miles, but after Preston speed began to build up, passing Oxenholme, ninety-one miles from Crewe, in 81¾ minutes, and the five and a half miles to Shap summit took just six minutes. Carlisle was approached with an average of 73.7mph from Shap summit to Penrith and then an average of 74.1mph from passing Penrith to the stop at Carlisle.

Once again, a good quick change of locomotive was made at Carlisle, with Caledonian No. 90 under the control of Driver Crooks away at 12.38. The stop at Stirling was dropped on this occasion and this may have led 'Baldie' Crooks to be careful at first, as there were no water troughs on this stretch of the line and a 150-mile non-stop run without water was about half as long again as most locomotives would have run on a full tank of water. The time to Stirling was actually two and a half minutes slower than Tom Robinson had managed with No. 78 the previous night with one carriage more. Nevertheless, speed rose as Perth approached and the train drew in to the station at 3.07½am, no less than twenty minutes earlier than on any previous occasion, having covered 449.9 miles from Euston in just 427½ minutes at an average speed, including stops for locomotive changes, of 63mph. At 3.09½, the locomotive change was completed and Driver John Soutar took the train away with what might be described as another 'veteran' of the races, Lambie 4–4–0 No. 17. The 89.7 miles to the Aberdeen ticket platform took just eighty and a half minutes and the train arrived in Aberdeen itself just two minutes later at 4.32am. The 540 miles had taken 512 minutes at an average speed of 63.3mph. One advantage of this early arrival was that mail aboard the train was early enough for the first morning delivery.

The East Coast had shown what it could do, but the West Coast had shown that it could do even better. How the East Coast companies must have rued taking Conacher's advice. Records are only set to be broken, after all. It was also true that the West Coast performance on the night of 21/22 August had been not as good as the previous night, leading many to believe that the 20/21 August had seen the West Coast at its peak.

Chapter 11

Outcome

The West Coast's startling performance shook the East Coast companies in their various headquarters at Edinburgh, York and King's Cross. True, they must have expected a riposte by the West Coast companies, but not one on such a scale, especially since the West Coast route was the longer one. It was also true that the East Coast record on the night of 21/22 August was against a poorer performance by the West Coast than on the night of 20/21 August.

There was no immediate reaction from the East Coast. The racing had stopped, as far as they were concerned, on 22 August. A week-end's reflection changed some minds at least.

On the morning of Monday, 26 August, Conacher wrote to Sir Henry Oakley showing that he at least had changed his mind. He still maintained that he shared 'to the full' Sir Henry's opinion about 'the childishness of the whole business', but did not want what he regarded as 'improper use being hereafter made of the West Coast achievement.' He was, in short, 'quite prepared to run another train as much like theirs as possible, when I have no doubt we could again shew our superiority.'

Conacher went on to write that he had used the newspaper accounts to assess just how the West Coast had managed such a sparkling performance, and had come to the conclusion that they had been able to run seventeen miles in eight minutes less time because they had gained an advantage through having a lighter load and fewer stops, as well as high speed in certain stages of the journey. His lengthy letter looked at ways of saving time, with four minutes less between London and Grantham, another five minutes saved between York and Newcastle, and another four minutes saved north of the border. He also wanted to omit stops.

Looking at the record of the races, one is struck by how little the managements of the East Coast companies seemed to know about actual performance on the line. Nowhere does any of the East Coast companies seem to have had a footplate inspector riding in the cab of one of their racing locomotives, let alone an observer on one of the trains. The lacklustre performance between King's Cross and Grantham does not seem to have struck home, nor the easy running after Dundee. The problems of water supply that seem to have inhibited performance between Newcastle and Edinburgh were nowhere mentioned. Admittedly, one solution, that of an extra tender, would have added much weight and could probably have been ruled out as a result. King's Cross, so keen to send spies to Euston in the hope of discovering the next move by the West Coast companies and the Great Northern in particular, did not send a 'spy' on any of the West Coast 8.00pm departures.

Oakley was in Dublin when Conacher's letter arrived and so could not reply until 28 August. He had also taken the time to consult with the North Western's chairman. The two men agreed that there should be no resumption of racing. Oakley wrote:

> We think here, if we were to begin again, the North Western must necessarily follow, and then the competition in speed must be fought out to the bitter end ... I am not much concerned by the empty honour won by the North Western as the fact of their reducing the weight of their train is a practical confession that on equal terms they would be unable to compete with us.

In short, the East Coast was to run to arrive in Aberdeen at 6.25am, and while the West Coast continued to advertise a 7.00am arrival, they felt that they were gathering the lion's share of the traffic. The races were seen as impractical, as the trains were far too short to be viable. This was a fair point, but the West Coast preferred to run with four bogie coaches, weighing in total around 95 tons, while the East Coast usually ran with six carriages, but of these five were six-wheelers, each much lighter than a bogie carriage, of which two were brake vans, while the sole bogie carriage was a sleeping car, so that the total tonnage was about the same, as was the passenger capacity.

Oakley's view was also that there should be no agreement with the West Coast on journey times as there had been at the end of the 1888 races to Edinburgh. In another letter to Conacher, he wrote that the West had been behind them the previous evening 'as they must be, if they are to run ordinary trains. When they shew a disposition to retreat, I should listen and fix the time of arrival with due regard to our more favourable distance. But I would rather not agree at all.' More than this, Oakley also felt that the East Coast companies had been freed from the agreement to run at the same time to Edinburgh.

Oakley was far from being a lone voice. Similar feelings about racing were felt along the road at Euston. George Neele had retired at the end of July, before the races had their final frantic ending, and he was clearly happy to be out of it, as he later wrote.

> Now there was nothing to be gained by the arrival at 6.25 or 6.30 in Aberdeen. The hotels were not open for their regular work; the discomfort of unprepared breakfast tables, or the accompaniment of dusting damsels in the coffee room, were travellers' annoyances rather than conveniences. The hour earlier into Aberdeen was a drawback rather than a benefit. However, at the end of July it ceased to be any part of my duty, and fell to the lot of my successor, to watch the daily morning reports showing how we had kept our time at Carlisle; how our allies had done their work to Aberdeen and whether our rivals had kept ahead of us or whether we had scored a success.

This was not the last word on the matter. This time it was not a resumption of the races to Aberdeen, but the decision to set a new record for a non-stop run.

On the night of 22/23 August, the LNWR had set a speed record between Euston and Carlisle, running the 299 miles at an average speed of 65.3mph, including stops. This was a world record over the distance. One Sunday, 1 September, the LNWR set out to show that the run could be completed non-stop.

For the record attempt, a special train was organized, leaving Euston at 8.45am, headed by a three-cylinder compound, No. 1305 *Ionic*, with a load of 151 tons, while the locomotive tender was modified with special wire supports so that coal could be stacked higher than usual. For the record attempt, *Hardwicke's* crew of Driver Ben Robinson and Fireman Wolstencroft was chosen. All went well and the run was completed at an average speed of 51mph and an arrival at Carlisle at 2.38pm.

Throughout the races, Rous-Marten had been reporting on developments for the *The Engineer*, and on 30 August 1895, the journal had this to say:

> The graphic articles from the pen of Mr Rous-Marten which we have published render it unnecessary that we should here say

anything concerning the events of the railway race which has just been terminated. But much remains to be written on certain aspects of the race concerning which the most extraordinary mistakes have been made by correspondents of the daily press. There is, too, some reason to believe that a section of the general public has regarded the race as a dangerous and almost criminal transaction. Mr John Burns, MP, has excelled himself in wild denunciation of the railway companies, and has drawn a lurid picture of the perils and sufferings of drivers and firemen, which only needed a small substratum of truth to be a really pathetic piece of oratory. It seems that Mr Burns has been riding on an engine in the United States and found it hard work, and a little alarming. We are not surprised. The experience of any man who rides on the footplate of an express locomotive for the first time is rather startling, but it is not necessary that as a result he should rush into print. But Mr Burns is by no means alone. Many other worthy people seem to regard with dread an attempt to accelerate communications with Scotland. It is just possible that a few words from us may tend to comfort and reassure these gentlemen. No lady correspondent of the daily press has yet expressed her fears. Possibly the racing spirit that induced the old lady to give her cargo of hams to the captain of a Mississippi boat to enable him to make more steam and beat a rival still beats in the female breast in this country. We have been repeatedly told that the race to Scotland is dangerous; that the men in charge of the train are overworked; that the speed is so tremendous that the passengers' health must suffer; that there is no time to avoid collisions; that the risks of running off the line, breaking the rails, bursting up the engine, breaking bridges and so on are simply enormous. All this is an admirable and instructive way in which history repeats itself. We can almost see some of the correspondents of the daily press copying their letters from old newspapers and reviews. In 1830, and one or two succeeding years, anything that has been written during the past couple of weeks was written and printed. The modern terrorist* has nothing new to say on the subject. All the fine old crusted stock arguments have been trotted out. We admit there has been one omitted. We have not heard a syllable

*By 'terrorist', the journalist clearly means someone who is an alarmist and causes panic through being overly anxious, rather than the modern meaning of a saboteur.

about the risk of suffocation, of which such capital was once made by opponents of railways; but this is a small matter ...

One gratifying result of the race will be perhaps to silence the boasting of the American press. The far-famed Empire State Express has been thoroughly beaten ...

Some things still have not changed. The ignorance of many journalists of the daily press, some of whom confuse trains with locomotives, persists, except that of course they now have the broadcast media joining them!

The races had seen an increase in the average speed for the journey from London to Aberdeen from 45.2mph to 63.2mph between 15 July and the morning of 23 August. The arrival time had gone from a convenient 7.35am to an unnecessary, except for the mails, 4.32am.

There was no question that the West Coast had won, for even when the East Coast shortened and lightened its train and removed calls from the schedule, the West Coast still outshone them, despite having the longer route. The highest average speed was on the West Coast. The 'race' fever did not seem to penetrate all the way down on the East Coast, from the management to the footplate or to the station platform. Perhaps keeping three companies in line was more difficult than simply having a partnership of two companies? It is also clear that the poor alignment and gradients between the Forth and the Tay also had an impact on the East Coast performance, as did the many single-track sections approaching Kinnaber Junction.

On the West Coast in particular, the races had a beneficial impact, at least for a period, with the summer timetable for 1896 showing many improvements on that for 1895. In 1896, McIntosh introduced his Dunalastair-class for the Caledonian Railway, introducing a completely new standard of performance that would certainly have given the West Coast an advantage had racing resumed. On the other hand, the North Eastern Railway allowed Wilson Worsdell to build two new locomotives, both 4–4–0s and numbered 1869 and 1870, which could fairly be described as 'racers', with 7ft 7in coupled driving wheels, larger cylinders and larger fire grates than the M-class so much in evidence the previous year.

Despite the prophets of gloom, the races of 1895 had not produced a single accident, although a clear warning of what could have happened was not long in coming.

On 13 July 1896, the 8.00pm Euston to Aberdeen was double-headed, but neither driver had worked the train before, nor driven an express not scheduled to stop at Preston. The station had a sharp curve at the northern end with a 15mph speed restriction, which the two drivers took at 50mph, derailing the entire train. In a derailment, much depends on the quality of the rolling stock and also whether or not any obstacle is struck by the carriages, and in this the North Western's luck held, for just one passenger was killed. Had earlier types of rolling stock been in use, the carriages could have broken up with greater loss of life.

While this accident was clearly the fault of the two drivers, who had made a serious error of judgement, it was also a failure to ensure that experienced drivers were not allocated to such a crack express. Today there would have been a 'pilot' – a driver familiar with the road – to see them through safely.

While the track was realigned to reduce the risk of a repeat of the accident, the main outcome of this was that, without any fanfare, the Anglo-Scottish schedules were eased until mile-a-minute running became a distant memory and eventually the East and West Coast companies reverted to their agreement on timings to Glasgow and Edinburgh of eight and a half hours, with Aberdeen taking much longer. It was not to be until the 1930s that significant improvements were to be made.

There was, of course, that outsider, the Midland Railway. In 1901, the Midland Railway and North British Railway produced a schedule for the 9.30am from St Pancras to arrive at Edinburgh Waverley at 6.05pm, just ten minutes ahead of the 'Flying Scotsman'. This in itself might not have worried the Great Northern and the North Eastern Railways too much, but for the fact that timekeeping on the Midland was erratic. The Midland trains all too often arrived late at Carlisle, and the fear was that the junction at Portobello might become the new Kinnaber as the signalman exercised his discretion over which train would be given priority on the many occasions when it was foreseen that the Midland train would be running late. The only solution was for the 'Flying Scotsman' to be accelerated so that it reached Waverley before the Midland train.

Thus it was that on the first day of the new timetable, 1 July, the 'Flying Scotsman' reached Waverley at 6.02pm, thirteen minutes early, while the Midland train, as expected, was late, although by just a minute, arriving at 6.06pm. The newspapers seized upon the story and tried to stir up interest in a new railway race, but it soon became clear that the excitement of 1896 could not be revived. During the first week, the 'Flying Scotsman' was early every day, arriving at 6.02, 6.03, 6.09, 6.07, 6.09 and 6.06, while the Midland was late every day, arriving at 6.06, 6.21, 6.15, 6.19, 6.12 and 6.14, showing that on three occasions it could indeed have interfered with the timekeeping of the 'Flying Scotsman', had the East Coast companies been prepared to let it run to time.

Chapter 12

Railways become Fashionable Again

The end of the races in 1895 was unlamented except for a few enthusiasts, and perhaps one or two of those working for the East Coast companies, who felt thwarted by the final victory of the West Coast. Perhaps they even felt cheated, as if the West Coast companies should have known when to stop.

Then, as now, the railway press described much of the reporting in the general press as 'amateurish' and 'uninformed'. A cynic might suggest that the general press were hoping for something dramatic to come out of the races, such as a serious accident, but that did not come until after the races were over (a year later, as we have seen). It does show the potential for disaster in the over-hasty approach towards Edinburgh at Portobello, where the speed limit was remarkably similar to that at Preston, but the potential for severe damage and loss of life and limb was greater given that the line was on an embankment with a bridge over a busy road.

The outcome of the accident in 1896 was a great deal more caution, and travel between London and Scotland became not only more cautious, but, some would say, also more sedate.

However, some voices were calling for the speeds attained to apply more widely to the regular express trains. *The Railway News* was amongst those that wanted higher speeds to be the norm rather than unusual. On 24 August 1895, the newspaper reported on 'The Race to the North – Close of the Struggle'. The lengthy piece amounted to a vigorous defence of the railways, and especially their remaining in the private sector, for it had been some years since nationalization had first been mooted and there were many who were working hard towards that end.

The directors and managers of some of our railway companies must be influenced in a very large degree by a burning desire to illustrate the lofty and sublime precept of returning good for evil. Parliament, representing more or less accurately the opinions of the public, has done all in its power to exact greater work for less pay from the railway companies, and traders and others who derive such vast benefits from the system, are forever combining and agitating against what they call the railway monopoly. Heedless, however, of all the undeserved attacks and unwarranted abuse which is heaped upon them, the companies are ever striving in a spirit of restless rivalry to outbid each other in their claims for the patronage of the travelling public. They do not compete, as in the case in America, in the commonplace, and happily obsolete, form of 'cutting' rates and fares; but seek by constantly adding to the comfort and accommodation of their patrons; by adopting all the latest appliances for safe and efficient working of the railways; and increasing the speed of their trains, to secure new business. Smitten on one side by their enemies in and out of Parliament, they show no resentment, but continue – with a perseverance and an energy which should command the highest approval and sympathy of all who can appreciate the lofty sentiments involved in the struggle going on in the railway world – to return good for evil. Parliament and the public had never asked the railway companies to run their trains between London and Aberdeen, a distance of 540 miles, in as many minutes. This, however, is what has been accomplished by the trains on the East and West Coast routes of Scotland. Talk as wildly as they may of railway monopoly, neglect of public interest, and growth of dividends, even the most rabid opponents of railways must admit the existence of keen competition among the railway companies. The statement of Lord Stalybridge to the North Western proprietors, that they cannot be left behind in the 'race', is a clear indication of the undercurrent of rivalry which exists between the companies, and which is none the less active and severe because it does not take visible form in the eyes of the public.

Practically, there is no reason, apart from the question of profits, why railway trains should not run at the speeds now advertised in the journey from London to Aberdeen by the two rival routes. The speed of 60 miles an hour is constantly exceeded on many portions of the leading railways. More than forty years since we remember to have travelled with Brunel from Bristol to London – 120 miles – in two hours. If all trains were to travel at these high rates, local and goods traffic would, however, come in but for a small share of the benefit of the railway system. As to the matter of the cost at which these relatively high speeds are attained, that is a point upon which further experience may be necessary before deciding whether the returns to the companies justify the additional working charges which are involved. On one matter at least, the proprietors may feel perfectly satisfied, and that is the splendid condition of the permanent way and rolling-stock which enables such feats in railway travelling to be accomplished.

This is an interesting assessment, especially by modern standards. In short, the second paragraph argues that higher speeds are possible every day, if the extra cost can be justified, then goes on to explain that running a high-speed railway, for that is what it is all about, could mean neglecting the needs of local traffic and the 'trader'. This is the justification today for building high-speed lines and leaving local and suburban trains, and rail freight or goods trains, to the traditional network. Even when four tracks are available and can be justified, there is considerable loss of efficiency if trains travelling in excess of 150mph are to share the same routes as those of necessity travelling less quickly, either because they are heavy freight trains with poor aerodynamics, or local trains constantly accelerating away from a stop or braking towards another.

The first paragraph also makes it clear in a long-winded manner that too many regarded the railways as a monopoly, although the writer did not agree. As mentioned much earlier in this book, the railways were often seen as having a monopoly, at least locally, despite the multitude of companies, and this led to some comparing the iron road with the public highway, especially when at first many railways were meant to be open to anyone who wanted to run a train. This led to the railways being brought into the concept of nationalization, of state ownership, even though the first example of this was in another form of communications altogether, the telegraph system. In due course, with nationalization, the railways were to mark the change from the state providing a service, such as the Royal Mail, to the takeover of a functioning business, or businesses.

The difference has to be, of course, that there was at the time no alternative to the Royal Mail unless one could afford to send a servant or an employee as a courier. There were other options than the railways. The canals still existed and, until the outbreak of the Second World War, there were coastal liners capable of carrying between six and 300 passengers on routes that rivalled the railways. The coastal liners enjoyed their heyday in the Edwardian period, with many lost during the First World War, and the years of the Great Depression accounting for many more, but while they survived they often provided a lower cost option to the railways. They also ensured many fewer changes, which is perhaps why they survived longest on routes between Great Britain and Ireland.

The truth was, of course, that if one was fortunate enough to live somewhere such as Edinburgh or Aberdeen, or Birmingham or Manchester, or even Southend, one did benefit from competition between railway companies. Indeed, until the early years of the twentieth century such competition existed between London and Plymouth, until the Great Western shortened its route with a 'cut-off' that gave it the clear lead, but competition continued at Exeter. In short, the railways were local monopolies that competed with their neighbours at the edges of their operating area. That being the case, the poverty of the two largest railway companies between the two world wars meant that Southend did not get what it really wanted: an electric railway to link the Essex resort to London.

Perhaps the real point is that private enterprise companies, especially those watched as closely by Parliament and the press as the railways, were more amenable and more easily influenced than state enterprise, or the lack of it.

Profitability

The period of the races was not an easy time for the railways. There had been industrial disputes in the mines and trade had been affected, although in 1895 it was recovering. The Edwardian era was a period of prosperity for the railways generally, although oddly enough not for the Midland Railway or the Scottish companies.

Looking at the main protagonists in the races, we can see that in 1912, the London & North Western paid a healthy 6.5 per cent, and even in Scotland there were dividends, with the Caledonian paying 3.75 per cent, although the North British had struggled to pay 3 per cent on its preference stock and 1 per cent on its deferred stock. The Midland, famous for the comfort of its trains, was not too well rewarded for its care, with just 2.5 per cent on its preference stock and 3.87 per cent on its deferred stock, but by contrast there was a dividend at 6 per cent on the North Eastern and the Great Northern paid 4.37 per cent.

There is a feeling that the more efficient railways enjoyed well-deserved profits, while the others struggled even during a period of prosperity, but one must remember that interest rates were far lower at the time than for most of the late twentieth century, so even 3 per cent compared well with the Post Office savings accounts. The Midland may have suffered because of its poor timekeeping and the poor productivity arising from too many small locomotives and too much double-heading of trains as a result.

The Scottish companies suffered because of a low population density over most of their area of operations. Whatever might be the impression of the North British, the Caledonian seems to have been efficient. A clue to the difficulty of running railways efficiently in Scotland came when, after the First World War, the government produced a white paper on rationalizing the railways. The outcome was grouping in 1923, with more than a hundred companies merged into just four, but the original plan had been for seven companies, one of which would be a Scottish company. This plan was amended after representations from Scottish business groups, who argued that a company based in and operating solely in Scotland would have to charge higher passenger fares and have higher freight rates than a trans-border operation. The result was, of course, that there were two trans-border companies, the London Midland and Scottish Railway, always known as the LMS for London Midland Scottish; and the London & North Eastern Railway, or LNER (the ampersand was dropped very quickly, although it did appear on a few locomotive tenders shortly after grouping). These were, of course, the natural successors to the West Coast and East Coast companies respectively.

Racing Again?

As one would have expected, the London & North Western Railway and the Caledonian Railway were both merged into the London Midland Scottish, as indeed was the Caledonian's rival, the Glasgow & South Western Railway, and the rival to both the West Coast and the East Coast companies, the Midland Railway. On the other side of the Pennines, and the other side of Scotland, all three of the East Coast companies, the Great Northern, the North Eastern and the North British, were merged into the London & North Eastern Railway, LNER.

Of course, it could never be quite as neat and tidy as that. The Midland's partner north of the border was the North British, although it also used the Glasgow & South Western to reach Stranraer in the south-west of Scotland for the packet service to Larne in Northern Ireland, where the Midland owned the Northern Counties Committee, the former Belfast & Northern Counties Railway, ownership of which also passed to the LMS.

While the restrictions on passenger services during the First World War were far less than those imposed during the Second World War, there were reductions in services as trains became less frequent and heavier, while making more stops. By the time of grouping, many of the wartime restrictions had been reversed. Nevertheless, one major problem that was not tackled immediately, even after grouping, was the artificially lengthened journey times between London and the major Scottish cities adopted in the late 1890s as a result of the last 'races', and which were simply badly outdated by 1923, but still allowed to persist for some time longer.

In fact it was not until 1932, some thirty-seven years after the end of the 'race' to Aberdeen, that the East Coast route was accelerated. There were some ridiculous situations in the meantime. From summer 1923, the night sleeper from King's Cross to Edinburgh Waverley took just seven and three-quarter hours, making it half an hour faster than the day's 'Flying Scotsman'. When Nigel Gresley introduced corridor tenders in 1928, allowing non-stop running between London and Edinburgh, the train kept to the same eight and a quarter hour schedule, so the average speed was just 47.6mph! The sheer nonsense of this was underlined by the fact that the following train, which made four stops, also took exactly the same time!

Despite this, in 1923, the LNER was Britain's fastest railway, with the 44.1 miles between Darlington and York on the East Coast route being run at an average speed of 61.5mph. The same high average speed was also to be found between Leicester and Nottingham in former Great Central territory. This distinction was short-lived, as in summer 1923 the Great Western accelerated its service from Cheltenham to run at 61.8mph between Swindon and Paddington.

The next significant step forward was on 11 July 1927 when the LNER inaugurated the world's longest non-stop railway service by running the 268 miles between King's Cross and Newcastle Central in a scheduled five and a half hours. Leaving King's Cross at 9.50am, the train headed by A1 Pacific No. 4475 *Flying Fox* reached Newcastle on time at 3.20pm, giving an average speed of 48.7mph. An even better performance was achieved on 14 July when No. 2569 *Gladiateur* (sic) managed the same down run in six minutes less than the schedule. Five locomotives were assigned to the service, three from King's Cross depot, including *Flying Fox*, and two from Gateshead, of which *Gladiateur* was one. The speeds achieved were not tremendous, even by the standards of the day, but these were heavy service trains rather than speed record breakers and the schedule was one that had to stand the problems of everyday operation. The achievement lay in running non-stop, with the train running as an advance portion of the 'Flying Scotsman' on Mondays, Thursday, Fridays and Saturdays, when demand was at its heaviest.

The following year, through non-stop running between King's Cross and Edinburgh Waverley started, setting a fresh record for distance with 392.7 miles, but not for speed, as this was an average of just 47.6mph, with a following train making four stops taking the same time. Despite this, the start of the service on 1 May 1928 was accompanied by a civic send-off at both ends of the route, with the trains leaving both termini at exactly the same time, 10.00am. On arrival at King's Cross, the LNER's chairman, William Whitelaw, was there to greet the footplatemen of the arriving train, while at Waverley, senior officers of the Scottish Area were present.

Services were accelerated in 1932 and again in the years that followed, but a major step forward came in 1935 with the introduction of the 'Silver Jubilee', running on weekdays between King's Cross and Newcastle Central in exactly four hours, with a stop at Darlington in each direction. This train was Britain's first streamlined train, with a stud of locomotives assigned to it and painted in the same silver livery as the carriages. Named to celebrate the silver jubilee of King George V, it provided people in the north-east with the opportunity of a return trip to London within the day. The through average speed was 67mph, but between London and Darlington, over the 232 miles the average speed increased to 70.3mph, at the time the world record for a non-stop run of more than 200 miles. Always anxious to remind the world that it could trace its ancestry to the first railway, the Stockton & Darlington, the LNER made much of the fact that it was celebrating its 110th birthday!

Until the 'Flying Scotsman' became a non-stop service, the LNER lagged behind the Great Western's 'Cornish Riviera Express', which made the longest non-stop run in the British Isles between Paddington and Plymouth, a distance of 225.7mph with an average speed of

54.8mph. The best the LNER could do was the 188.2 miles between King's Cross and York at an average speed of 53.8mph.

Many of the railway companies had congested approaches to the London termini, but both King's Cross and Euston were particularly bad examples of this. The situation at King's Cross was made worse by the number of double-track bottlenecks between London and York, with the tunnel and viaduct at Welwyn being problems that persist to this day. The only way of coping with this problem was to run the fast expresses in groups, with several trains leaving mid-morning, then again at lunchtime, in the late afternoon and late evening. This would have been a problem on some railways, but the very long distances covered by many LNER expresses meant that the type of clockface departure favoured on the Southern was not necessary, although eventually this was introduced for shorter distance trains. An example of how this worked in practice comes from the summer timetable for 1939. After a three-hour interval from the departure of the 'Flying Scotsman' at 10.00am, there were departures from King's Cross to Newcastle at 1.05pm, Edinburgh at 1.20pm, West Riding at 1.30pm and Harrogate at 1.40pm, followed by a long interval until 4.00pm before more fast services departed. The gaps between these 'flights' of departures was needed for slower trains and especially freight traffic.

The growth of paid summer holidays also meant that the summer season began to expand, although it was not as long as today, while the pressure at weekends meant that many of the expresses had to run as several parts, each in fact a full-length train running closely behind the principal train. This worked well as long as no problems were encountered, but the schedules had no slack left for any delays, and so if a locomotive or carriage failure occurred, punctuality suffered and normal working and good timekeeping could not be resumed until the following day.

As noted earlier in the races to Aberdeen, punctuality was a problem for the LNER just as it had been for the East Coast companies. The trains from London to Scotland were classified as 'inter-area' as they passed through three areas and at first the Aberdeen trains passed through four areas until those for southern and northern Scotland were combined. As late as 1928, a table in the *London & North Eastern Railway Magazine* showed punctuality as improving, but slowly, for the first four weeks of each year, inter-area trains running an average of 3.9 minutes late that year, having run 4.9 minutes late in 1926, the year of the General Strike, and 5.1 minutes late in 1927. These trains were the least punctual in the whole company.

One problem for the LNER was that it decentralized its management, and so the problems of coordinating several companies became the problems of coordinating several areas. Many railwaymen believe that the key to punctuality is to have the same general manager in charge at both ends of the route. This the LNER did not do, in contrast to the LMS, which became very highly centralized, but with regional control centres inherited from the Midland Railway, which had also struggled with punctuality.

New Rolling Stock
The LNER soon showed that it wanted its prestige expresses to be the most modern in terms of both the locomotives and the carriages. The 'Flying Scotsman' got new carriages in 1924, then again in 1928 and 1938, as well as being amongst the first trains to enjoy new rolling stock once the Second World War ended when it was updated again in 1946.

Some improvements were planned, but others came by accident. The LNER inherited the contract between the former Great Eastern and the Pullman Car Company, which had not proved as successful as the GER's general manager, Henry Thornton, had hoped. A suggestion by the Pullman Car Company that a service between King's Cross and Harrogate would also be popular for business travellers to and from Leeds and Bradford failed to inspire the LNER's passenger managers, but fortunately they were overruled by the chief general manager, and the service started on 9 July 1923, running via Harrogate to Ripon and Newcastle. Not all of the new services using Pullman carriages were so successful, but the 'Queen of Scots' proved to be another success, with new rolling stock provided in 1928.

On grouping, the LNER inherited more than 200 restaurant cars, including the GER's Pullmans. Most were for first-class passengers on the longer-distance trains, but even at the time more casual eating was beginning to appear in addition to the company's practice of providing a five-course *table d'hôte* menu for a set six shillings. An innovation was the introduction of the buffet car in 1932, initially serving just drinks and sandwiches, although hot meals were later introduced. One advantage was that it became possible to provide catering for travellers getting off, or on, at intermediate stops. The move was so popular that by 1939, the LNER had 306 restaurant and buffet cars, with some longer-distance expresses, such as the 'Flying Scotsman', having both conventional restaurant cars and buffet cars.

Another modern feature introduced in September 1930 as an experiment was the provision of radio in certain carriages, for which the passengers hired headsets. The early trials were between King's Cross and Leeds, but the service did not seem to become widespread, although whether this was because of reception problems or the availability of rolling stock is unclear. Perhaps other passengers found the sound that did leak through the headsets worn by their neighbours annoying!

Even before grouping, Gresley had started to build articulated sets, reducing the weight of the train and also improving the ride. The rolling stock incorporating this feature was usually in two or three-car sets, but a five-car dining set introduced in the early 1920s was also the first to use electric cooking, with a marked improvement in safety compared to the gas stoves that were in general use. The move to articulated sets was not without some controversy in the operating department, or in the case of the decentralized LNER, operating *departments*, as a fault in one vehicle resulted in the whole set having to be withdrawn. This, of course, is no different from multiple unit working today, but at the time it was seen as a major disadvantage.

The needs of third-class passengers were also catered for in other ways. Until 1928, all sleeping cars were first class, but that year the LMS and the LNER introduced third-class sleeping cars, although initially these were what would now be described as couchettes, easily convertible for day use and with four passengers per compartment. The management of both railways were concerned that the facility would result in some loss of passengers from the traditional first-class sleepers. Standard third-class fares were charged with a supplement of seven shillings, for which a pillow and blankets were provided. Within a few years, new third-class sleepers were introduced with permanent beds, with either two or four berths per compartment, with first-class compartments having just one berth. The sleepers became increasingly popular despite the years of the Great Depression. From this time onwards, most of the passengers using sleeper compartments were in third class, showing how sensible it had been to introduce third-class sleepers, and to ensure that proper sleepers with fixed berths were provided rather than 'couchette-style' accommodation. Even with the higher speeds achieved by both the LMS and the LNER in the late 1930s, only a sleeper service could provide an early arrival and assure a full day's work.

In 1938, from Euston, there was a sleeper every night except Saturdays that departed at 7.20pm and reached Aberdeen at 7.10am the following morning. This was stately progress compared with the races of 1895, as was the following 7.40pm departure, which arrived in Aberdeen at 7.40am. This shows, however, how the traffic had grown and the trains were far heavier with up to sixteen carriages, with a restaurant car as far as Crewe on the 7.40pm. These trains also divided with carriages for destinations such as Inverness and Oban. Later sleeping car trains, leaving at 10.50pm, but with access to sleeping berths from 10.35, were really for Edinburgh and Glasgow passengers, who otherwise would have arrived at their destinations at an uncivilised and inconvenient early hour.

Over at King's Cross a similar regime existed. The 7.25pm departure, 'The Highlandman', actually served Inverness, which it reached at 8.45am. The next sleeper away was the 7.40pm, 'Aberdonian', which reached the Granite City at 7.20am. A restaurant car was attached as far as York. The 'Night Scotsman', departing at 10.25pm, conveyed passengers 'north of Edinburgh only' reaching Aberdeen at 11.12am. The following 10.35pm, unnamed, reached Edinburgh at the convenient hour of 7.30am, in good time for breakfast at the North British Hotel (now the New Balmoral). Then there was the 10.45pm, but that only went as far as Newcastle, reaching it at 5.10am, with the assurance that passengers could remain in their sleeping berths until 8.00am!

Towards the Modern Railway Carriage

Naturally the LMS inherited the West Coast joint stock, which included magnificent twelve-wheeled dining and sleeping cars, and the twelve-wheeled corridor coaches built for the appropriately-named 'Corridor' train that ran from Euston to Aberdeen, Edinburgh and Glasgow, and back, and the boat train sets for Euston–Liverpool (then the Cunard Line's port for its sailings to and from the United States and Canada). The rest of the passenger carriages inherited from so many different companies were so varied and often so dated that the policy, as with the locomotive fleet, had to be one of 'scrap and build'. The passenger rolling stock policy was left in the hands of R.W. Reid, who had been the Midland's carriage superintendent, and took up the same position with the LMS.

Although the LMS experimented with articulated passenger carriages, these did not enter volume production. There were innova-
tions, however, and as large picture windows became more popular
by the end of the 1920s the LMS was building carriages of this pattern,
having built ones with side doors shortly after grouping. These had
small opening windows above the main picture window, which itself
could be dropped, with rotating vanes that could be set by passengers
to either face or trail the passing airstream – no doubt the true reason
for the adjustment was that the carriage could be run in either
direction.

One question was that of open saloons versus compartments.
Despite its admiration for much that was American, the LMS maintained that many of its passengers preferred to have the privacy of a
compartment rather than an open saloon, but both types were built for
both first and third-class passengers, although on many trains the
open saloons were marshalled next to the kitchen cars to allow them to
be used as dining cars.

Carriage parts were prefabricated to speed production, so that the
main production line was engaged in final assembly only and the
more detailed work was handled away from it. 'All-steel' carriages
(the roofs and window frames were still made of wood) were the next
step, easing mass production but also, from 1929 onwards, to reduce
the demand for mainly imported timber and provide work for the steel
industry, which was hard pressed by the Depression years. This, after
all, was what Churchill had in mind when in 1929 he had removed the
railway passenger duty on condition that the money be capitalized by
the railways and invested in modernization, and later the government
provided low interest Treasury loans for the same reason. Considerable orders for new carriages were placed outside the company with
independent carriage builders, as the company's own works could not
keep pace with the demand.

All-steel was an apt description, but the interiors were trimmed with
wood, and in later years the LMS had a small notice advising passengers of the type of wood used and its place of origin, which was
always within the British Empire. Comfort was of a high order, with
seats padded and sprung, which was a step forward, as some of the
older pre-grouping companies had used horsehair. The new first-class
compartments had just four seats, so that everyone had the prized
corner seat, but the first-class open carriages had one and two abreast
seating, as one would find today. In 1930, windows were made deeper,

while the overall carriage length was stretched to 60ft, not to increase capacity but to improve comfort, so that third-class compartments went from 6ft between partitions to 6ft 6in, while first-class went up to 7ft 6in. The improvement was temporary, and clearly too expensive at a time of financial hardship, and carriage lengths soon reverted to 57ft. The third-class compartment was reduced to 6ft 3in, a compromise.

When Stanier became CME in 1932, the changes continued. In contrast to his work on locomotives, he did not bring GWR ideas with him for carriages, which would have been a backward step. No longer were window frames and roofs made of wood. These too were made of steel and window frames were rounded, while sliding window ventilators were placed in the upper part of the main window for the first time. Comfort for the third-class passenger on the main line expresses was improved when compartment carriages had their accommodation reduced from eight seats to six, with armrests and reading lights, so that they almost rivalled first-class on some companies. In theory, the armrests could be lifted to allow two more passengers to sit, but once comfortably seated few were kind enough to do this.

The later LMS rolling stock provided the basis for the British Railway's Mark 1 passenger carriages, whose demise is much missed in these days of high window sills and seats not aligned with windows.

Faster Trains
Comfort was an important factor in the renewed competition for passengers between London and Scotland, as were on-board services such as hairdressing and the provision of secretaries on some trains. There was no attempt to return to the railway 'races' of 1888 and 1895, but the LNER forced the LMS into action when the East Coast company announced late in 1936 that it would celebrate the Coronation of King George VI with a streamlined express running between London and Edinburgh. It took just weeks for the LMS to put one of its new, but unstreamlined, Pacifics, *Princess Elizabeth*, on a high-speed run from London Euston to Glasgow Central with a rake of seven carriages, far fewer than the locomotive would normally have handled. On 16 November 1936, *Princess Elizabeth* completed the journey in just five hours, fifty-three and a half minutes for the 401.4 miles. Even better, the following day she did the return run, but with eight carriages in high winds and heavy rain in just five hours forty-four and a quarter minutes, giving an average speed of 70mph throughout the

journey. This was an achievement, as even then it was known that railway rolling stock had 'drag' and that high winds could also adversely affect performance.

'Over 800 miles in two consecutive days at a mean average speed of 69mph with an average load of 240 tons!' the *LMS Magazine* told its readers in a story by-lined 'By One Who Took Part'. The story was in fact too late for the December issue, so while it was accorded a brief mention, readers had to wait until January 1937 for a more detailed account.

The record was short-lived, even though the 'One Who Took Part' saw it as a milestone in railway history.

Six weeks after the stirring events of those two days, the achievement is one which has passed into railway history, and which now comprises a mass of dynamometer-car and other records in course of analysis. Yet those who were privileged to take part in these epoch-making journeys from London to Glasgow and back in less than six hours for the 401½ miles, and those who saw the train flashing through the countryside, will long treasure memories and incidents serving vividly to recall this wonderful demonstration of speed on the steel highway. Not, indeed, since the famous 'Races to Scotland' of the eighties and nineties has the West Coast Route known such a drama as that of this racing train and her gallant crew pitted against the clock –and, on the return trip, against the weather too.

Despite this, the record is not remembered as a major event in railway history, not least because even better was to follow once the first of the streamlined locomotives, *Coronation*, emerged from the works. On 29 June 1937, a test run was conducted between Euston and Crewe with the locomotive 'reined-in' between Euston and Stafford, leaving Euston at 9.50am and running to the timetable, but the locomotive was then given her head, reaching 114mph past Maddeley to reach Crewe just before noon. On the return, the 270-ton train left Crewe at 1.55pm and covered the 158.1 miles in just 119 minutes to arrive at Euston at 3.54pm, giving an average speed of 79.7mph start-to-stop. This compared with a booked time of 144 minutes for the Crewe–Euston leg.

The achievement earned the LMS front-page news coverage, with the tabloid *Daily Sketch* giving over the whole of its front page for the story. The newspaper photographs of *Coronation* give the impression that she had a load of just two carriages, but the official account in the *LMS Magazine* makes it clear that the load was eight carriages.

In the down direction the 158.1 miles Euston to Crewe were covered in 129 minutes 46 seconds, at an average speed of 73mph, start to stop. The maximum speed between Whitmore and Crewe was 114mph (as recorded by the speed-recorder on the engine), while speeds of 112.5mph were maintained for a full mile and 106.5mph for five miles. The maximum speed of 114mph is the highest yet recorded in this country and the highest (with steam traction) in the Empire.

That was not surprising as none of the Empire countries had anything that would qualify as a high-speed railway. At the time, French railways did not have their reputation, gained many years after the Second World War, for high-speed record-setting, and it was only in Germany and the north-eastern United States that speed records were being set, but with diesel traction. Perhaps more interesting was that the locomotive had a speed recorder, as the LMS did not provide speedometers on its engines, something that was to come back to haunt the company in an accident later on.

Despite this, the LMS did not schedule the 'Coronation Scot' as tightly as it could have done. Perhaps this was to ensure a robust timetable with on-time arrivals, or perhaps it was a concern for safety with the train running at high speeds every day, or even a concern for passenger comfort. Or, perhaps, it was being parsimonious, with concerns over the consumption of coal and additional wear and tear on the locomotive and rolling stock. This was one weakness of the class, for there were just five locomotives with streamlining, and as it was claimed that this made a significant difference to speeds of more than 70mph, tighter schedules could not have been maintained if a non-streamlined locomotive had to be substituted.

As for the LNER, on Sunday 3 July 1938, during a series of high-speed brake trials on the main line between Peterborough and Grantham, the opportunity was taken to make an attempt on the world speed record for railways using the A4 locomotive No. 4468 *Mallard*. Although the load was far less than a full train, it was no lightweight either, with three twin articulated carriages from the spare 'Coronation' set and the company's dynamometer car, making seven vehicles in all with an empty weight of 236.5 tons, or 240 tons with officials and equipment aboard. *Mallard* was chosen because she was one of three A4 locomotives to have the Kylchap exhaust arrangements, which included a double blast-pipe and chimney. The decision to find out how fast the locomotive could run with the seven-vehicle load seems to have been almost a spur of the moment decision, and it is notable that no one from the *London & North Eastern Railway Magazine* was aboard, leaving the publication to reproduce an account from *The Railway Gazette*.

> *Mallard* took her rake of carriages through Grantham station at just 24mph because of permanent way work, and then accelerated to almost 60mph over the next 2½ miles up a rising gradient of 1:200, eventually reaching almost 75mph over the next mile-and-a-half to Stoke summit, again over a further stretch at 1:200. Descending Stoke Bank, the speed rose to 116mph, and then to 119mph, and then crossed the 120mph mark where it stayed for the next three miles, reaching a maximum of 126mph. The locomotive maintained a speed of between 123mph and 126mph for nearly two miles. The record-breaking run was then curtailed as the opportunity was taken to conduct a brake test from such a high speed and the train was approaching the curve at Essendine, which also included several sets of points, and it was thought unwise to take these at such a high speed.

This was a greater achievement than generally realized, not only because it has never been beaten anywhere, but also because, far from being specially prepared, *Mallard* had worn valves and was driven hard by a driver, Driver J. Duddington of Doncaster, known for thrashing his locomotives. Had she been properly prepared and all valve clearances correct, the record might have been set even higher. As it was, those on the footplate could smell the machinery as it overheated and the locomotive needed major workshop attention afterwards.

Many claim that the record could have been beaten by the Coronation Class, and others claim that other railways abroad could have done better, but we shall never know. Nevertheless, the former East Coast and West Coast companies, now the LNER and LMS, settled on the former running between London King's Cross and Edinburgh Waverley in six and a half hours, while the latter took six and a half hours to Glasgow. It was the LNER that ran non-stop trains using water troughs and even had corridor tenders so that the footplate crews could swap over without the train stopping, while the LMS was content to call at Carlisle. The 10.00am departure from King's Cross, the 'Flying Scotsman', reached Aberdeen at 8.00pm having taken ten hours, including a lengthy call at Waverley.

To improve performance between Edinburgh and Aberdeen, and especially over the difficult lines in Fife, the LNER's Chief Mechanical Engineer, Sir Nigel Gresley, built six P2 2–8–2, or Mikado, locomotives, Nos 2001 to 2006, with the later examples having the same streamlining as the A4 class. The earlier ones were converted to have the same appearance. These were all rebuilt as Class A2/2 in 1944.

The railway companies were aware of the importance of streamlining and of the impact that strong winds could make on locomotive performance. It was not just the locomotives, as the aerodynamic drag of the carriages was also important, perhaps even more so than that of the locomotive on a lengthy train. The National Physical Laboratory at Teddington had conducted trials using model locomotives, but plans to produce a rival to the French locomotive testing plant at Vitry-sur-Seine, which actually tested real locomotives, came to nothing, despite Gresley and Fowler of the LNER and LMS respectively collaborating and deciding on a site at Crossgates, near Leeds, in 1930. The outlook for the economy was bleak and so the project was shelved until better times came – but they never did.

It is impossible to assess how well the streamlined trains did for the railway companies. Many believe that they were in effect 'loss-leaders' due to poor utilisation of costly locomotives and rolling stock, as well as high staffing and maintenance costs, not to mention the extra fuel consumed by high-speed running and the need to maintain track at the highest standards. The problem could have been that the speeds were not in fact high enough for streamlining to make a significant difference in fuel consumption, and that it was not until the era of the high-speed train, aka the InterCity 125, that streamlining really began to have a beneficial effect.

Interestingly, neither the Great Western nor the Southern indulged in streamlining, with the former simply adapting two locomotives in 1935, No. 5005 *Manorbier Castle* and No. 6014 *King Henry VII*, adding partial streamlining consisting of a bullet nose to the front of the smokebox and coverings over the external cylinders, as well as air smoothing over a number of items and a wedge front to the cab. The Southern confined itself to the air-smoothed Bulleid Pacifics of the Merchant Navy, West Country and Battle of Britain classes. These were the two most profitable railway companies amongst the 'Big

Four', but they were also the least dependent on freight and the ones most active in pursuing diesel traction in the case of the GWR and electrification in the case of the Southern.

Many have since suggested that the railways should have abandoned setting steam railway records and instead followed the Germans and Americans in developing higher speed diesel locomotives and multiple units, such as that used on the German Hamburg and Berlin express, inevitably called the 'Flying Hamburger'. This ignores the fact that between the two world wars, the railway press featured many articles discussing the possibilities of diesel or electric trains, alongside others looking at the future for steam. Steam was still an advanced technology at the time. Both the LMS and the LNER had great hopes for high-pressure steam locomotives, but while both companies produced prototypes, the example on the LMS was withdrawn after a serious accident and the LNER example was seen as a maintenance nightmare. There was another consideration that had reared its head even before the outbreak of the First World War: the strategic implications of relying on imported fuel. This had led the pre-First World War Admiralty to be cautious about how many of its major warships were oil-fired. With vast reserves of coal, steam remained an attractive option, even if expensive.

When it did happen, after nationalization, no railway system in the world converted from steam to diesel and electric as quickly as Great Britain. Unfortunately, the infrastructure was not converted at the same time, and diesel locomotives were maintained in the same filthy sheds as steam engines, with an adverse effect on reliability.

Even before the demands of another war and then nationalization, the thirties were in fact a less competitive era. Three of the 'Big Four' companies, the Great Western, the LMS and LNER, had even agreed to pool their freight collection and delivery services outside of London and in some cases pool receipts in order to cut costs. The Southern was only excluded from these arrangements because it carried so little freight, and except around Exeter had little overlap with any other company. The 'Big Four' sometimes collaborated when buying bus and coach companies whose operational area overlapped those of two railway companies, and perhaps the greatest example of collaboration came when they bought the nationwide road haulage companies, Pickfords and Carter Paterson.

Chapter 13

Wartime and Nationalization Slow the Railways

All ideas of speed came to an end with the start of the Second World War. Once again the railways were taken over by the Railways Executive Committee, although for the time being they were left in the hands of their proprietors.

On the eve of war, the Minister of War Transport, as the Minister of Transport had become, moved quickly to seize control of the railways on 1 September, using powers granted to him under the Defence Regulations Act 1939. There was considerable delay in fixing the basis on which the railways would be paid, with the state taking all of the receipts and allocating what it regarded as a suitable sum to each of the four main line railway companies and London Transport on a pre-determined basis. There was little real negotiation, with the government hinting at acceptance or nationalization. The inclusion of the London Passenger Transport Board in the scheme was opposed by the 'Big Four' railway companies who believed, wrongly as it turned out, that passenger traffic would slump in wartime, and that as the only all passenger operator, London Transport would become a liability for the others. It certainly meant that the allocated funds would have to be spread around more thinly.

The state also decided what resources could be made available in terms of raw materials and manufacturing capacity to keep the railways running. This was not nationalization in the true sense of the word, but it was a bureaucratic straight jacket, although it must be borne in mind that the control and direction of labour, raw materials and manufacturing capacity applied to the entire economy and not just the railways.

Despite the haste to grab control of the railways, there was considerable delay in finalizing the means of working. The system of state control meant that the railways effectively became contractors to the government, with all revenue passing to the government, which then allocated a share out of a pool, which was set at a guaranteed £40 million. The LNER share of the pool was fixed at twenty-three per cent, while the LPTB received eleven per cent; the GWR received sixteen per cent, the same as for the Southern Railway, and the LMS thirty-four per cent. The difference between the LNER and the LMS was interesting as the total track mileage of the two railways was not as different as the pool share suggested. These percentages were based on the average net revenues for the companies and LPTB in the three years 1935–37, which the government regarded as the standard revenue for each company. Once the guaranteed £40 million had been paid, any balance was allocated to the five train operators on the same percentage terms up to a maximum of £3.5 million. After this, the arrangements became complicated, since if there was a further balance, the revenue over a total of £43.5 million would be divided equally between the government and the pool until the pool total reached £56 million. At this stage, if the revenue share allocated to any of the companies then exceeded its standard revenue, the figure the companies had been expected to earn annually at the time of the grouping, the excess would be shared out proportionately among the other companies.

Costs of maintenance and renewals had to be standardized, while the cost of restoring war damage would be met up to a total of £10 million in a full year. Privately-owned wagons were also requisitioned by the Ministry of War Transport, and the individual companies had to meet the costs and revenue attributed to the wagon owners out of their share of the revenue pool.

This was a 'take it or leave it' type of agreement, with the government leaking threats of nationalization if the companies failed to agree, although these were officially denied. The years in question had not been good ones for the British economy, although 1938 had been worse and the railways had had to work hard to get the government to recognize this. The difficult economic conditions that had prevailed for almost all of the inter-war period had meant that none of the railway companies had ever achieved the standard revenues anticipated by the Railways Act 1921, the measure that authorized the grouping. The best that can be said for the deal was that the government was anxious to avoid inflationary pay claims from railway employees, and no doubt anxious to ensure that it did not play a part in war profiteering, since it was likely to be its own single biggest customer, but the inescapable fact was that the railways were having their revenues more or less fixed while costs were bound to rise as they struggled to meet the increased demands that wartime would place upon them. Placing an upper limit on the cost of making good war damage was another instance of either political expediency to keep the unions quiet, and the Labour Party within the wartime coalition government, or simple naivety since normal insurance measures were not available in wartime.

Nevertheless, within little more than a year, the Ministry of War Transport reneged on the original agreement and left the railway companies to pay for war damage out of revenue. The fixed annual payments were also changed, with the provision for extra payments dropped so that any surplus would be taken by the government, which generously also offered to meet any deficit, which was an unlikely event given the demands placed on the railways. The new deal provided for the following annual payments:

London & North Eastern Railway = £10,136,355
London Midland & Scottish = £14,749,698

Restrictions Begin to Bite
At first, the instruction was given on all railways that, on an air raid warning being given, passenger trains were to stop and passengers allowed to alight and seek shelter if they wished, after which the train would continue at a maximum speed of just 15mph. As the full extent of the bombing became clear, and air raids became very frequent, traffic was slowed to an unacceptable extent, and the instruction was revised, with trains allowed to proceed at 25mph from early November 1940. The danger of a derailment to a train running on to bomb-damaged track at high speed during an air raid was obvious, but away from the most heavily bombed towns, many drivers took a chance and ignored the speed limit, guessing that the risk of bomb damage was relatively low.

On 11 September, drastic cuts were imposed on train services, meaning great hardship for passengers since, although the late holiday traffic had virtually disappeared, normal business travel was still at virtually pre-war levels. Like the railways, some large companies had dispersed, especially those with strategic importance such as the shipping lines, but it was not possible for everyone to do so, as apart from business considerations, the number of suitable venues outside

London and other major cities was limited. The many smaller businesses and professional practices remained in London. After the uproar that followed, normal services were reinstated on weekdays from 18 September.

Nevertheless, this was simply a temporary reinstatement and indicated nothing more than that the blanket reductions of 11 September had not been properly thought out in the short time available to the timetable planners. Wartime conditions meant that services had to be reduced, to save personnel, fuel and wear and tear, and to make trains and paths available for the military. New timetables imposing reductions in passenger services followed on 2 October, largely because of the considerable volume of the LNER's commuter network. On this occasion better allowances were made for peak period travel. Off-peak, most main line services lost their usual trains with the service halved, often running to extended timings as trains called at more stations. Nevertheless, the national maximum speed limit was increased to 60mph during October.

Catering arrangements were reduced. Pullman and buffet cars were withdrawn and restaurant car service ceased on most routes. These cutbacks must have once again aroused some public reaction and been regarded as too severe, for on 1 January 1940 Pullman cars reappeared, as did pantry cars and more buffet cars. There was considerable debate over whether sleeping car services could continue, but a number did, although for the ordinary traveller, the reprieve was short-lived.

On the London & North Eastern, the Edinburgh service saw the number of trains cut from fifteen to just eight, while the journey times for the 393 miles extended from a pre-war best of 390 minutes and an average of 466 minutes to 608 minutes. As elsewhere, the outbreak of war was followed by severe cuts to railway passenger services, partly to save fuel and manpower, but also in anticipation of immediate heavy bombing. These cuts were common to all of the railway companies and were far too severe. On 11 September 1939, the LNER issued a new timetable, cutting crack expresses and putting trains that could at best be described as 'semi-fast' in their place. The public uproar was such that the Railways Executive Committee relented, and on 2 October a new timetable showing improved services was published. Even so, there were fewer trains and these were all slower than those for the same period of the previous year, while amenities such as restaurant cars were missing and there were just three sleeping-car trains. The 'Flying Scotsman' was replaced by a 10.00am to Edinburgh that did not reach its destination until 7.30pm, adding three hours to the pre-war schedule. Performance was not helped by lengthy refreshment stops, such as fifteen minutes at Grantham and eighteen minutes at Peterborough, needed to compensate for the lack of catering facilities on the trains. This was a backward step, to the early days of railway travel before dining cars appeared. Passengers did not descend on a dining room as in days of old, but instead had a trolley service on the platforms, and there were none of the multi-course meals enjoyed by Watkin!

The LMS naturally did not escape the cuts. The service from Euston and St Pancras to Glasgow was cut from twelve trains in 1938 to six in 1939. The average journey time was increased from eight hours six minutes to ten hours four minutes, but the fastest in October 1938 had been just six hours thirty minutes for the 401 miles. Inverness took sixteen hours twenty-six minutes from London instead of thirteen hours, while the number of trains was halved from four to two.

Despite the looming shortage of everything, including paper, yet another new timetable was issued on 4 December, with more trains and with the return of a number of restaurant cars and buffet cars. Refreshment stops were also much reduced.

There was constant debate over whether sleeping cars should or should not be withdrawn. Many felt that passengers needed this facility, which was once again restricted to first-class only, but others argued that extra day carriages provided better use of the limited number of trains being run. From December 1942, these carriages ceased to be available for civilian passengers, although a skeleton service was maintained for those travelling on government business.

While mainline trains retained first-class accommodation, after a period of reduced catering facilities, on 22 May 1942, all catering facilities were withdrawn from trains on both the LNER and the LMS.

Post-war, services started to get back to normal, although very slowly at first. There was much bomb damage to be repaired, but even worse than this was the limited maintenance of track and rolling stock during the war years. There were numerous temporary speed restrictions; the number of carriages and locomotives available for service was much reduced, not so much because of the military making exceptional demands for equipment to use overseas, as this had been less than during the First World War, but because of the arrears of maintenance.

Despite these problems, the shortage of materials, including new track, continued after the war, with the four mainline railway companies unable to get even their normal peacetime requirements filled, when, of course, their needs were far heavier than they had been in 1938. Despite their best efforts, much work remained to be done when nationalization overtook the railways on 1 January 1948. In short, it took some time before even the pre-war schedules could be restored. It was not until the summer of 1954 that the 'Flying Scotsman' once again carried passengers between Edinburgh Waverley and London King's Cross non-stop in six and a half hours. The magnificent A4 streamlined locomotives could have cut this, as many observers found that an on-time arrival remained possible even after delays of ten or fifteen minutes en route.

Nationalization removed the competitive edge between the East Coast and West Coast trains. This was ultimately to the railways' disadvantage, as their glamour image also disappeared, only to be revived briefly when the East Coast rolled out the InterCity 125 high-speed train, with its Mk.III carriages and Class 43 power cars. In co-ordinating services and reducing waste, the railways fell behind at a time when the long-distance motor coach could provide greater economy, and the aeroplane greater speed. The motor car and the motorway brought a new dimension to the travel scene. Travelling by air, one could spend a day on business in Edinburgh, Glasgow or London and be home again that night, and while this is now once more possible by rail, the amount of time that can be spent at the destination is still slightly less, in the author's own experience, when travelling by train than by air.

Not for nothing are the glory days of railway travel in Great Britain seen as those between 1895 and 1939, with the years of the First World War and of the General Strike excluded.

Bibliography

Given the wide scope of Britain's railway history, it is not possible to provide a complete list of books on the subject. Old copies of *Bradshaw's Railway Guide*, originally published monthly, are illuminating when they can be found, and the reprints by David & Charles are better value than the originals, now collectors' items. A good sample of books would include at least some of the following:

Allen, Cecil J., *Titled Trains of Great Britain*, Ian Allan, London, 1946–1967.

Beaumont, Robert, *The Railway King: A biography of George Hudson railway pioneer and fraudster*; Review, London, 2002.

Bonavia, M.R., *A History of the LNER*, 3 vols, George Allen & Unwin, London, 1983.

Christiansen, Rex, *A Regional History of the Railways of Great Britain: Volume VII – The West Midlands*, David & Charles, Newton Abbot, 1973.

Hamilton Ellis, C., *The Trains We Loved*, Allen & Unwin, London, 1947.

Hoole, K., *A Regional History of the Railways of Great Britain: Volume VI – The North East*, David & Charles, Newton Abbot, 1965.

Jackson, Alan A.; *London's Termini*, David & Charles, Newton Abbot, 1969.

Joy, David, *A Regional History of the Railways of Great Britain: Volume VIII – South And West Yorkshire*, David & Charles, Newton Abbot, 1975.

McKean, Charles, *Battle for the North – The Tay and Forth Bridges and the 19th Century Railway Wars*, Granta, London, 2006

Neele, George Potter, *Railway Reminiscences*, 1904.

Nock, O.S.; *A History of the LMS*, 3 vols, George Allen & Unwin, London, 1983.

—— *The Railway Race to The North*, Ian Allan, London, 1959.

Peacock, A.J., *The Rise and Fall of the Railway King*, Sutton, Stroud, 1995.

Smullen, Ivor , *Taken For A Ride*, Herbert Jenkins, London 1968.

Simmons, Jack, and Biddle, Gordon, *The Oxford Companion To British Railway History*, Oxford University Press, Oxford, 2000.

Thomas, John, *A Regional History of the Railways of Great Britain: Volume VI – Scotland*, David & Charles, Newton Abbot, 1971.

Wilson, C. David, *Racing Trains: The 1895 Railway Races to the North*, Sutton, Stroud, 1995.

Wragg, David, *A Historical Dictionary of the Railways of the British Isles*, Wharncliffe, Barnsley, 2009.

—— *The LMS Handbook 1923–1947*, Haynes, 2010.

—— *The LNER Handbook 1923–1947*, Haynes, 2011.

—— *Signal Failure – Politics and Britain's Railways*, Sutton, 2004.

Index